THE CRIME-CONTROL ESTABLISHMENT

THE AMERICAN ESTABLISHMENTS SERIES

EDWIN SCHUR, *general editor*

Each book in the AMERICAN ESTABLISHMENTS series examines a single, broadly defined "vested interest" in our society. The volumes focus on power and resistance to change in these American institutions, providing a radical reassessment of their future influence.

Isidore Silver, editor of this book, is an Associate Professor of Law at John Jay College of Criminal Justice.

THE CRIME-CONTROL ESTABLISHMENT

edited by ISIDORE SILVER

A SPECTRUM BOOK

PRENTICE-HALL, INC., *Englewood Cliffs, New Jersey*

Library of Congress Cataloging in Publication Data

Silver, Isidore.
    The crime-control establishment.

    (A Spectrum Book. American establishments series)
    1. Law enforcement—United States. 2. Crime
prevention—United States. 3. Narcotics, Control of—
United States. I. Title.
HV8138.S5   363.2′0973   73–21880
ISBN 0–13–192682–9
ISBN 0–13–192674–8 (pbk.)

© 1974 by Prentice-Hall, Inc.
Englewood Cliffs, New Jersey

A SPECTRUM BOOK

10 9 8 7 6 5 4 3 2 1

Printed in the United States of America

Prentice-Hall International, Inc. (*London*)
Prentice-Hall of Australia Pty. Ltd. (*Sydney*)
Prentice-Hall of Canada, Ltd. (*Toronto*)
Prentice-Hall of India Private Limited (*New Delhi*)
Prentice-Hall of Japan, Inc. (*Tokyo*)

Contents

THE CRIME-CONTROL ESTABLISHMENT

Introduction

ISIDORE SILVER

Is there a "crime-control establishment?" If there is, who (or what groups) comprise it? What precisely does it do and what effect upon the society does it have? Is it important that we understand that such an "establishment" exists, that it plays a vital role in our understanding (or, rather, misunderstanding) about that most persistent, most unsolvable, and most perplexing social problem of our time, "crime," and that its power and influence are increasing?

The thesis of this book is that there indeed exists a specific combination of men and agencies (mostly concerned with the subject of "crime control") whose activities—most often, for the worse—substantially shape public attitudes toward crime. Also, these agencies have the political capability to transform their views about "crime" and "crime control" into law and, more importantly, into law enforcement. Also, the activities of these agencies have created (and are continuing to create) a situation whereby a large number of our citizens have become or are becoming labelled as "criminals," and, thus, subject to police control and, ultimately, police repression. It is not necessary that there be a "plan" or a "conspiracy" among these agencies to achieve these questionable ends; the effects are frightening enough. If our national fear of "crime," our national willingness to condemn much human conduct as criminal, and our national unconcern with the social and economic causes of "crime" is suddenly abetted by a changed political atmosphere which increasingly relies on police control, the results may be serious, indeed calamitous.

It is important, therefore, that the reader, bewildered by the profusion and variety of "crime" and the apparent inability of our system to contain it, comprehend that neither he nor the society is the hopeless victim of overwhelming "natural" criminality; that our

1

"establishment" functions to perpetuate myths about "crime," to enact or help to enact legislation which "criminalizes" large areas of human conduct, and to create or reinforce in us certain attitudes about "crime" and "crime control"; that agencies in the criminal justice system, because they are political agencies, stand to "gain" something—either in economic, organizational, or prestige benefits —by engaging in certain conduct and encouraging the American people to believe that their conduct is right and effective. The reader cannot understand the possibilities for reform of the system, for the lessening of "crime," for the chance to rebuild our divided society, unless he is fully aware that the "criminal justice system" is run by men and institutions, many men, many institutions, often for their own ends.

The men and their institutions exercise power and use the authority of the State to facilitate such exercise; they may well believe that their exercise is both beneficent and productive. Whether or not we agree—and increasingly we appear to disagree—we must understand what they are doing and how they are doing it. I think that the exercisers of that power, who have largely failed to understand "crime," understand that crime cannot be entirely eradicated from any society, especially ours. But in trying to achieve such control, they have perpetuated the myth that man can be fundamentally changed by law and that the criminal law, with its penalties (though not rewards), is the best vehicle for attainment of the "noble end" of a harmonious, well-ordered society. You may not agree, but you should have the opportunity to assess for yourself just how much of our Criminal Law and Criminal Procedure are man-made and just what (and whose) interests they are serving. The "crime crisis" and the "crime-control crisis" felt by all of us is sufficient justification for the decision to undertake this inquiry.

II
THE MEANINGS OF ESTABLISHMENT

Before the nature and the role of this "establishment" can be fully understood, we must comprehend just what this critical term means, for "crime control" is not a single activity dominated by our unified group. The term "establishment" was first popularized (facetiously) in 1961 by Richard Rovere and, after about a decade of overuse, has faded somewhat in public consciousness.[1] It is difficult to define the term precisely—and even more difficult to apply it to "crime control." It could mean either one of two things —(a) a group of individuals sharing certain values who control or powerfully influence a given activity or (b) a group which is *recognized by the public* as having authority to establish certain values on behalf of the public in relation to that enterprise. Thus, for instance, there may well be a "foreign policy" or "foreign relations" establishment, the object of Rovere's initial analysis, but it is not widely known. The Foreign Policy Association may well supply Secretaries of State (Under-Secretaries to be more realistic) and may well staff sundry committees and commissions that review and make recommendations concerning our national foreign policy, but this "establishment" is virtually invisible to the public.

Of course, Rovere would argue that any such stable group with a continuing effect upon a given enterprise (i.e., foreign policy) must be regarded as an "establishment," irrespective of public knowledge or interest. This is consistent with his definition: "a more or less closed and self-sustaining institution that holds a preponderance of power in our more or less open society." Given the term's shift in meaning since 1961, it is even conceivable that, in certain areas, there may be two "establishments," the apparent and the real, the former believed by the public to be dominant, while the latter may in fact be. Both groups may be somewhat interconnected, and the function of the "public" establishment may well be to conceal some quite unacceptable activities of groups who remain unknown and unaccountable. This is particularly true of "crime control" where certain sectors—police, prosecutors, the F.B.I. all *appear* to dominate. Although, as we shall see, the F.B.I. is a critical component of the real establishment, it is also a vital link in the connection between the "real" and "apparent" groups.

Ultimately, the meaning of "establishment" can only be made clear by analyzing the activity which it involves. The composition and role of the establishment may be more easily discerned in one enterprise than in another, for certain historical or political reasons. Thus, foreign policy, to continue with the original example, is a

[1] "Notes on the Establishment in America," *The American Scholar,* Vol. 30, Autumn, 1961 (pp. 489–95).

field about which the public demonstrates—and has traditionally demonstrated—only intermittent concern. Apart from knowing the role of the president himself, and perhaps that of an advisor of note such as Henry Kissinger, there is no deeper public involvement that would lead to a concern with both the issues and the groups which deal with them. The establishment does not seem to exist. In the realm of crime, where public concern and personal involvement is always high, more men and institutions appear to be authoritative, and their guidance is publicly sought.

Confusion about a crime-control establishment exists at yet another level. Crime, despite a generalized public fear, is essentially a local phenomenon (unlike foreign policy). Crime control has been traditionally a concern of local authorities, police, prosecutorial, judicial, and correctional (although, as we shall see, this is in the process of change). Clearly, the crime-control establishment cannot be easily located in a body such as the Foreign Policy Association or in highly coordinated private groups (such as top fashion designers, to choose an unobvious, but nevertheless real example).

The difficulty of identification is compounded by the fact that crime is such a widespread phenomenon in our society; so many groups participate in the formulation of the specific concerns of "criminal justice" that the whole enterprise appears to be random. Much—some observers say most—human conduct is encompassed within the broad definition of crime and it, at times, appears that any organized group which objects to some sort of activity can have it declared illegal and punishable under our continually expanding criminal codes. Religious groups may be interested in having adultery, prostitution, and abortion declared (or maintained as) crimes; businessmen may fear public disorder and argue for strict vagrancy laws; politicians fearful of threats to government may enact criminal syndicalist laws; and, finally, professional groups such as medical associations may think that certain health menaces (drugs, for instance) should be criminalized.

Pinning down the establishment becomes more difficult when we realize that American attitudes about crime (and enforcement) are shaped as much by tradition as by the activities of particular groups in society. While it is true that our traditions can be—and are—manipulated by groups to achieve their own ends, the simple force of these traditions is a formidable one indeed. The American heritage consists largely of an invincible belief that law is morally based, that all sorts of human conduct should be made criminal, and that the solution for our social problems lies in continuous criminalization of more and more conduct.

Also, tending to discount the existence of a relatively stable or fixed "crime-control establishment" is the very linkage between crime and politics. In a real sense, the crime establishment is synonymous with the political establishment. If the political establishment of the nation at a given time in history is anti-communist, or anti-radical, then the law enforcers will concentrate on the appropriate "public enemies." When the national mood and our political concerns change, then we concentrate on other allegedly hostile groups; the concern of the Truman and Eisenhower eras for Communism gave way, rather quickly, to Kennedy's war on organized crime and labor racketeering.

Since crime is a local phenomenon, and a local political phenomenon at that, the picture becomes more confused. The enemy is often a community enemy and its identity will shift with the political concerns of diverse communities. If Panthers carry guns into San Francisco courthouses in the sixties, then one of their most famous leaders can blithely run for mayor of Oakland in the seventies. As this is being written, the community of Madison, Wisconsin, elected a former student radical as its mayor. Of course, despite this peculiar example, we know that most communities, governed as they are by congeries of the leading businessmen and financiers, will tend to enforce those laws most appropriate to the needs of local establishments. The mass media and the use of it by Federal agencies may nationalize crime; when Communism is an important national issue, everybody seems to set up a "Red Squad."

Thus, it would appear that the very nature of the crime problem, its localism and its intimate connection to politics, may well defeat the notion of a single overall crime-control establishment. But, if we keep in mind both definitions of establishment—(a) an elite with real, albeit behind the scenes, power to influence policy and (b) a group of individuals or institutions which are perceived by the public as having the authority to define (and even create) crime and propose measures to deal with that definition—then other truths clearly emerge. History, both recent and long-range, demonstrates that the American people, insofar as they seek general definitions of crime and punishment, have looked to certain national institutions, especially to federal law enforcement agencies as authoritative. More importantly, those institutions have functioned as continuing sources of influence upon Congress and the executive to create new "crimes" and new law enforcement "anti-crime" weapons. As crime becomes a national concern, as federal jurisdiction expands, as federal and state law enforcement agencies increasingly cooperate to "fight" crime, the influence of these agencies will only increase. Clearly, they are the major components of the crime-control establishment.

III
IDENTIFYING THE ESTABLISHMENT

Of course, the prepossessing figure of J. Edgar Hoover traditionally dominated the American people's perception of both crime and punishment. For forty-eight years he headed the Federal Bureau of Investigation and dexterously built it into the most publicized, if not necessarily the most efficient, engine of law enforcement. His accomplishments run even deeper; almost single-handedly (and certainly single-mindedly), he created (or, perhaps, reinforced) certain images of crime. Those images were, for the most part, accepted—and acted upon—not only by that amorphous group, the people, but by other criminal justice agencies. For most of his tenure, he was almost a one man establishment.

Books, articles, and speeches flowed from the man or his ghost writers with unceasing, torrential regularity. He depicted the nation as menaced by various conspiracies, all designed to sap and destroy "Americanism." Some of these conspiracies overlapped; more often, they were separate and discrete ones. Generally, they were political in nature and ranged the (narrow) gamut from radical, anarchist, syndicalist (in the twenties) and communist (in the thirties and fifties) through Nazi and Fascist (during World War II) to Black Panther and Weathermen (in the sixties). At times, they were purely "criminal" and depraved—the Dillinger-type gangs of the thirties, juvenile delinquents in the fifties, and the muggers and rapists of the sixties.

The numerous contradictions in Hoover's (and his supporters') demonology were only rarely publicized. The F.B.I. and other law enforcement agencies were—and are—seen always as highly efficient and invariably successful, so that any such conspiracy should by all rights have been destroyed. Yet, it persisted over time. Of course, when some conspiracies abated—and this became obvious to even the most obtuse members of the public—new ones had to be created. The response was always a variant of: "No matter how successful we are, the conspiracy never really dies. It only goes underground and always seeks to rebuild its strength."

But Hoover was not the only federal law enforcer who took his case to the public. In the thirties, Harry Anslinger, Director of the then Bureau of Narcotics of the Treasury Department, managed to propagate the idea that various drugs, including marijuana, were socially dangerous (although the supporting rationales were contradictory and changed considerably over time). As Hoover encouraged enactment of criminal syndicalism laws, so Anslinger encouraged—and was even mainly responsible for—passage of our unbelievably harsh drug proscriptions.

The student of "establishmentarianism" must pause to ask at this point just whose interests were being served by the emphasis of the American people, and their acknowledged leaders, on the subjects so dear to the hearts of Hoover and Anslinger?

The question is required by the very nature of our problem. Establishments influence (or control) public policy; that policy is set by government. The clearest example of policy formation is Law. Of critical—though generally overlooked—importance is that "crime," "the criminal," and the other concepts we shall discuss are defined by the political organization of society. Crime is designated by Law, and the activities of the criminal justice system (those institutions which society has made responsible for identifying, apprehending, and dealing with those who have been thought to violate the criminal law) are, in part, regulated by Law—and Law is the creation of a political process. The legislature (or the United States Congress) acts as a political body when it enacts (or refuses to repeal) criminal laws; the executive is a political agent of the State (used in its classical sense to mean organized political authority) when he enforces the Law; and the judiciary is also political (in the same sense) when it judges individuals accused of violating the Law. The police, probation, parole, and other officials (generally serving the executive branch) are agencies also created by Law to serve legal functions and play legal roles. Since the law is the will of a political body, they are also *ipso facto* political agents of the state.

The concern of the intellectual discipline of Political Science and of our inquiry involves yet another (informal) meaning of the term "political." Politics, as used to analyze establishment activities, describes the distribution of benefits and harms within an organized society and provides the legal machinery to support such distribution. Men (and establishments) use the political arena (in its broadest sense, whether it means executive, legislative, judicial, or administrative) to attempt to arrange the distribution in their favor or in favor of groups they represent. This may be a perfectly acceptable process, so long as the rules of political combat are observed. The criminal law is one such arena, a very serious one—and the stakes are high for both the group or individual seeking to use it and the group or individual potentially harmed by its use. Often, the advantage sought in Law—even the Criminal Law—is material, often it is moral or ideological. Whenever a group succeeds in gaining the advantage, it has a form of Power. The question for Political Scientists—and for this book—to ask is whether any such groups are *consistently* able to secure the benefits of the Criminal Law or whether their exercise of power over power (the power of the State to compel obedience once a law is enacted) is temporary or incomplete (in that they may not be able to get all they want). Also, particular groups may only succeed in particular areas, so that their power, though considerable, is limited in scope.

Presumably, such successful groups (or, needless to say, individuals) will not only benefit by getting laws of their choice but will enhance their power because of the very existence of these laws. The Law itself is a source of authority (as judges well know) and, insofar as authority (the belief that someone is acting legitimately and not capriciously) is a source of Power, then a group is strengthened by success. As the old saying goes, "Nothing succeeds like success."

Thus, Law and Law Enforcement are the results of a political process (political in both senses of the term)—although not only of that—and should be studied as the Political Scientist studies any form of Politics. It is not enough to assume that the Law magically exists—that it comes from some undefined source or from the collective wisdom of the populace. Often, that source is to be found in the activities of men and groups who have, or acquire, a vested interest in the legal process.

Thus, the concept of "establishment" is in great part a political one, and we must ask the invariable political question—Who benefits? Men represent interests as well as ideologies, and though it has been assumed that Hoover and Anslinger, e.g., represented no interests, perhaps further critical examination of their careers will suggest more realistic views.

Although the F.B.I. and other government agencies are vital components of the establishment in question, we do not know which other groups clearly benefit from the activities of a Hoover or an Anslinger. We know that the *interests* of certain groups parallel those of our most eminent law enforcers. We know that labelling the labor movement as either criminal or at best susceptible to criminal activity helps business—or that it did so in the twenties.

We have no proof that there was a "hidden establishment" directing or at least influencing the overt one of Hoover and Anslinger. We know that Hoover cooperated with big business and that Anslinger's anti-drug crusade may have been of more than coincidental aid to the growing, in 1937 recently legalized, liquor industry.

The full story of the F.B.I. has yet to be told, for when it has not been engaged in wild publicity stunts, it has operated in comparative secrecy for decades. Hoover may well have influenced Americans about crime, but he did so through his writings, his stunts, and his often favorable press. In the '30s, captures of Alvin Karpis and "Pretty Boy" Floyd and the killing of John Dillinger impressed the public mind with the agency's predominant role in American law enforcement. That, in perspective, much of this bally-hoo was self-inflated and of only minor social importance is irrelevant, for it worked. Despite the Bureau's less than exemplary record in the '40s, it allegedly disposed of the internal Nazi and Fascist menaces and vigorously attacked the growing communist threat at the end of the decade—or such was the impression it wished us to believe.

IV
THE ESTABLISHMENT
AND THE PUBLIC

Since the American people have vague, confused, and contradictory notions about crime, the establishment is able to wield substantial power over public perceptions about the subject. The establishment has answers while the public has only questions and frustrations. To be specific, on April 4, 1973, the front page of the late City Edition of the *New York Times* contained thirteen news and feature items. Of these, six involved crime, criminal justice, and the administration of criminal justice. Even a superficial glance at the headlines should be sufficient to describe the bewildering and complex variety of events that are commonly lumped together under these rubrics. Thus, the second lead column headline informed a doubtlessly surprised public that INSURANCE FRAUD CHARGED BY S.E.C. TO EQUITY FUNDING and the opening lines of the story described the "Equity Funding Corporation of America," "once the darling of institutional investors," as the subject of investigations (a) "to determine whether insiders had engaged in illegal trading . . ." and (b) to ascertain whether it sold "alleged nonexistent insurance" (to other insurance companies). For any reader who may have been confused by the alleged arcane dealings of a major American corporation, the headline immediately below the Equity Funding revelation doubtlessly proved more familiar; it read LIDDY SENTENCED FOR DEFYING JURY and referred, obviously, to the endless Watergate case.

The third lead column announced that the United States Senate had approved "stiff mandatory prison sentences for nonaddicted persons convicted of Federal charges of selling hard drugs." Thus, sale of at least one-tenth of an ounce of heroin or morphine would require (assuming the bill were enacted) a judge to impose a ten to thirty year sentence; for a second offense, the sentence would be life, with no possibility of parole for 30 years.

Other prominent stories included the (spread over four columns) third in a series on New York City's juvenile justice system, while other stories recorded the introduction of a state master plan to build new and renovate old prisons, and a court denial of a sweeping attack on New York State's bail practices. Clearly, on April 4th, there was much for the reflective reader to brood about.

Of course, none of the stories were particularly startling or novel. Someone who, with reasonable diligence, had followed standard accounts in the *New York Times* and elsewhere, would know that the American system of criminal justice in general is in dire, if not terminal, condition.

On April 4th, he might have dismissed G. Gordon Liddy's contemptuous conduct in defying a federal grand jury as just another demonstration of the dirtiness of American politics. Since April 4th, however, he might have become properly indignant over the likelihood that considerable sums of money were spent (or authorized) by some of the highest government officials in the land to commit various crimes.

Our mildly informed reader may well have approved the United States Senate's vigorous demonstration that, once again, it is determined to stamp out the hard drug traffic in the United States. After all, heroin, he knew, was the major cause of property crime in the country and an increasingly important factor in much crime of personal violence. His beliefs—and those of the Senate—reflected the success of a sustained campaign by the Bureau of Narcotics to convince us that criminal penalties (ever-increasing ones at that) were necessary to deal with the drug menace. If the reader's memory were capacious, he might note that New York and the federal government already had severe penalties on the books for the crimes involved, and that they didn't seem to deter anybody.

The reader would have approved of Governor Rockefeller's prison plan and would have vigorously agreed that only 20% instead of the present 80% of all prison inmates should be confined in maximum security facilities. His eye would be caught by a front page reference to Attica, "the scene of a deadly inmate revolt and police assault in 1971," and he might have remembered that only one correction officer was killed by the inmates in that "deadly . . . revolt" and that the police assault required the killings of 29 inmates and 10 of their hostages. He probably would also have remembered the McKay commission's Attica Report—or at least summaries of it in the newspapers—which argued that Governor Rockefeller should have gone to Attica and that the assault was poorly handled, that many inmates had been beaten in post assault reprisals, and that the state police had lied to the Commission about their activities. He might have been mildly hopeful that the new proposal would finally solve the problems of inmate revolts for, he would admit, there were justifiable grievances, though they should have been settled without force and violence. He would not have questioned the underlying tenets of the prison system at all—probably in unconscious tribute to the fulminations of J. Edgar Hoover on the subject.

If our reader had then looked up as his commuter train from Westchester passed through Harlem, he would undoubtedly again have wondered just how all of those people could survive in that environment. He would have shuddered at the complexity of their problems—the substandard housing, the high unemployment rate, the incidence of narcotics addiction, the "welfare mess," and all of the rest. A part of him would have recoiled at the inhumanity of city life and he would admit that "there but for the Grace of God, go I"; another part of him would doubtlessly have shuddered at the possibility that stark hatred and desire for revenge might victimize him or a loved one in the city some day. How could we have made such a mess of things, he would ask. He would not know that the activities of the establishment (and its satellite, the whole crime-control industry, the police, the prosecutors, etc.) had as much, if not a greater, role in determining his preoccupations, as did all of the deplorable physical conditions he had observed and those social problems reflected in the headlines.

V

THE CHANGING (OR DEVELOPING) ESTABLISHMENT

There is nothing in the nature of establishments—especially of the one which now concerns us—that precludes growth and change. But though both may occur, certain other fundamental political and social changes clearly indicate that the problems previously mentioned will only deepen. Such growth in the establishment does not necessarily mean that the federal government itself will become an important crime fighter. It does not require an end to the power structures of local communities, analysis of which would teach us more about the significance of crime control than would a decade of reading sociological treatises. It does not require that the "common crimes," the F.B.I. Index Crimes, be transferred to the jurisdiction of the federal government.

Just as the general activities of the federal government in the 20th century often touch the lives of the citizenry more substantially than do the activities of the states, so, increasingly, does the federal criminal process. Both state social and welfare programs, as well as state criminal justice concerns, are modelled after, or are pale reflections of, their federal counterparts. All social services are now being seen as an integral whole: Welfare, health care, and unemployment are perceived as being national in scope, just as our economy transcends state lines. Increasingly, congress, the executive bureaucracy, or the federal regulatory agencies are either coordinating state efforts, providing minimal standards, or providing insurance for them by means of complicated financial schemes. While older concepts of "Federalism" (or the newer counterparts) dictate some—even much—deference to state initiatives in certain realms, the prospect is for continuing federal action of some sort (even if limited to a supervisory role). The host of recent anti-pollution legislation and the complicated relationship of state anti-pollution agencies to their federal counterpart provide only the latest instance of the public's reliance upon the federal government for a major role in meeting social problems.

Since "crime" is a major social problem, we should expect an increasing centralization of anti-crime activities in the federal government. Such has occurred, albeit with due respect to the federal principle. Both the states and the federal government have entered into major new areas of law enforcement in the 20th century. A major work would be needed to detail increasing federal government involvement with criminal activities once thought to be local, in areas such as gambling, drugs, bank robbery, extortion, and riot. The rationales have been both reasonable and persuasive; in general, they parallel those which justify increasing federal intervention into other formerly local state activities. The society is complex, crime is interstate, the use of the telephone and the automobile have rendered state boundary lines superfluous (and conveniently provide a constitutional rationale for federal criminal jurisdiction), and the activities of organized crime are nationwide (if not worldwide) in scope and effect. In addition, the treaty power of the United States has been used to increase the number of local activities which can become criminalized under federal law (federal drug control laws are partially based upon international treaty obligations) for congress has the power to enact statutes pursuant to treaty as well as to constitutionally granted jurisdiction.

Of course, the laws are so framed that not only members of interstate organized crime rings are included; everyone who commits the prohibited act is subject to prosecution. The "Rap Brown" Act penalizing interstate travel to commit riot is another clear example of a jurisdictional power shift. Federal standards for wiretapping and bugging are contained in the Omnibus Crime Control and Safe Streets Act of 1968, and the evidence is that only the approbation of all branches of the federal government for such practices (the Supreme Court has held that controlled tapping and bugging are constitutional) has spurred the states into action. The activities of the Law Enforcement Assistance Administration have done much to *sanction* state anti-crime activities. That agency (whose funding substantially increases each year) in theory only operates to fund state sponsored projects designed to "improve" the quality of criminal justice. The agency is presumed to be value free in that money is awarded to projects recommended by independent state boards. While many of the projects are of dubious value (many of the state board members are practicing members of local criminal justice establishments), they are not the result of any federal government ukase, though an indirect effect caused by federal public relations activities on both local establishment values and the projects that may be shaped by them is not ruled out. Of course, the next step— perhaps a logical and inevitable one, given the abuses of LEAA funds—is for the creation of "federal spending standards" to guide disbursal of federal monies. Ironically, this may occur just because of the heavy criticism (generally offered by liberals) of the often bizarre nature of approved local projects. But it may occur here, as it has in other areas of federal spending (although this is now lessening), because congress wants to say how federal monies should be spent.

The process of increasing federal involvement in state criminal justice activities is an historical one, and the current activities against organized crime and drug use only constitute an acceleration of a shift of power which began with the assumption of F.B.I. jurisdiction in Mann Act and stolen automobile cases. The process will doubtlessly continue, although its form may well consist of providing subsidiary, rather than primary, police and other services to the states.

Another powerful factor adding weight to the effectiveness of federal action on subjects of allegedly local interest is the fact that the federal government does exercise local jurisdiction on federal enclaves within the states and, most particularly, in the District of Columbia. Although the practice of "preventive detention" has not yet been adopted by the states, its mere existence in the District may well serve as an example and an impetus to future local action, especially if the District (containing many of the same "criminal elements" as predominate in our largest cities) appears to be successful—more successful than the states—in combatting crime.

There are key individuals and key institutions in the federal government, beyond those already mentioned, which may legitimately be labelled "establishment" in the crime-control fight, whose influence is quite extensive. Men such as Senator John McClellan, the Chairman of the Senate Permanent Investigations Subcommittee and his chief adviser, Robert Blakey, the Notre Dame law professor who drew up most of the Omnibus Crime Control and Safe Streets Act of 1968, have already demonstrated considerable political power. President Johnson signed that Act reluctantly, in recognition of that power. A future president may well have fewer qualms than did Johnson when confronted with future crime control legislation. The vagaries of American politics are unpredictable, but the apparatus and the rationale are there, as is the inclination of the states to allow the federal government to take the lead.

The influence of the Federal government has also been great in contributing to a shift in the public's perception of crime away from the traditional acts against persons and private property to a concern with "political crimes." Federal political trials such as those of the Chicago Seven (for interstate travel to commit riot and for "conspiracy"), Benjamin Spock (and three others) for conspiring to abet violations of the selective service laws, Daniel Berrigan (for conspiring to destroy draft board records), and Daniel Ellsberg (for espionage and other crimes in relation to the copying and distribution of the Pentagon Papers) have emphasized the federal government's concern for penalizing the acts of political opponents. Numerous state trials—with mixed results—of radicals and Black Panthers have followed in the wake of these federal political prosecutions. Of course, the phenomenon of the political trial is not new in American law, but the spate of prosecutions undertaken recently indicates that government generally, and the federal government in particular, is quite willing to label its political opposition as criminal, thus to stigmatize it with the most odious form of symbolic condemnation possible. The communist of yesterday, the anarchist of the twenties, and the assorted bugaboos of yesteryear have been replaced by an assortment of contemporary menaces which justify the extension of the federal police power (and emulation by the states), and these "public enemies" will undoubtedly become the subjects of yet newer laws and newer practices which will, in turn, further extend federal criminal jurisdiction and further politicize American law. They also will foster the growth of a community of interest among various levels (and various components) of law enforcement.

Also, a concatenation of diverse interests is clearly apparent in our drug law enforcement policies. The simple political fact is that (a) large groups of people, relatively well-educated, liberal or radical people, have not only been labelled criminal, but have become subjects of police records and (b) marijuana laws have been often and incontestably utilized to harass *political* opponents of particular regimes, both national, state, and local. Criminal convictions (or even arrests) have the effect of preventing (or seriously impeding) the ability of a whole segment of our youth from entering active political life and attempting to initiate and foster political change. Those who have acquired police records subject themselves to continuing police surveillance, to police control. We do not have internal passports as do totalitarian countries which perpetually attempt to keep an eye on the activities of the citizenry; but we have almost its equivalent, police records which can be, and are, increasingly centralized.

Although doubtlessly much police (and other criminal justice) activity in the realm of marijuana possession is "innocent"—of political overtones—much may well be designed to achieve specific political ends, to stifle what many may believe is the growth of a youthful, radical, political movement, or even to harass well-known apolitical figures. Clearly, this one aspect—the use of marijuana laws to remove from political circulation known and acknowledged leaders—is verifiable. Although the social sanction for such activities may lie elsewhere (in our outmoded value schemes, for instance), the political uses of the marijuana laws proceed apace.

The leadership of the F.B.I. and the Narcotics Bureau, a matter of historical record, has, as a result of their processes, been supplemented by the rise of agencies such as the Law Enforcement Assistance Administration and Federal Strike Forces. Both old and newer components of the establishment have been furnished with increased weaponry and new communications and record keeping innovations—all tending to centralize crime control power. The combination is—or is becoming—an increasingly unified one, and that cohesiveness can only grow and, in turn, pull more institutions (local and state police, for instance) into its orbit. The prospect for the crime control establishment is, then, internally bright and almost limitless; its effects upon the rest of us are something else again.

I
The federal crime-control
establishment

The Federal Bureau of Investigation is, by all odds, the quintessential example of the success of the crime-control establishment in American life. From a discredited, tiny, and almost comically malevolent agency of the Justice Department heavily involved in the Teapot Dome scandals of President Harding's administration, it grew under the aegis of J. Edgar Hoover into a mammoth national police force with a prestige approaching the legendary. Its jurisdiction (and, inevitably, its funding) expanded rapidly in the thirties and forties to encompass numerous, formerly local, crimes such as kidnapping and auto theft. Its incessant publicity mill justified such expansion and, ultimately, both the American people and the Bureau's political allies in congress (and occasionally the Executive branch) came to regard it as the most efficient law enforcement agency in the world. The story is almost incredible, yet grotesquely logical, given our national propensity to fear "big" crime, Red Menaces, unruly labor movements, the revolutionary rhetoric of groups such as the Black Panthers, and other symptoms of the moral breakdown of the country. The Bureau, under Hoover, was certainly the right agency at the right time in history; it took advantage of the chaos of the new world of the mid-twentieth century and assured those of us who were fearful that we could return to an older, safer time—if we would, of course, unleash the forces of law and order against various demons.

Toward the end of his life, J. Edgar Hoover granted an interview to *Nation's Business,* and that prestigious publication faithfully hewed to what most Americans seemed to believe about the F.B.I. Thus, Hoover

> has molded the Federal Bureau of Investigation into a model
> law enforcement agency and kept it that way. . . .
>
> "FBI" became an abbreviation that commanded the respect
> and cooperation of citizens. "G-Man" became a nickname feared
> by criminals and subversives.

Hoover in January 1972 staunchly argued that the Bureau's investigative jurisdiction had been increased to 185 matters because of "Congressional enactments, Presidential directives and orders of the Attorney General . . ." and that expansion of his domain was unsought—indeed even, at times, opposed.

Hoover's jurisdictional modesty is contravened by Max Lowenthal's detailed and, for now, definitive study. Using essentially public sources such as congressional hearings and Bureau reports, this careful, scholarly lawyer wrote the *Federal Bureau of Investigation* in 1950, and little written since then has matched its quality. Indeed, the spate of materials on the Bureau contributed in recent years by Fred Cook and the Committee for Public Justice, among others, is little more than an update of Lowenthal's work and a confirmation of the fact that the Bureau is indeed a powerful—if not *the most* powerful—force in shaping American attitudes toward crime and crime control.

In this Post-Watergate moment of relief, it would be appropriate to note that Lowenthal was not concerned with the question of the Bureau's role as shaper of public attitudes but with (to quote from his preface)

> the extent to which a federal police agency is needed for the
> curbing of crime; the functions appropriate for such an agency;
> the investigation of non-criminal matters; possibilities and meth-
> ods of controlling the police agency; the impact of a central
> police force on American life.

The fundamental question underlying these particular issues is, of course, "does the Bureau present a threat, present or future, of a police state independent of democratic political control?", and the Watergate revelations, if anything, document the extent to which the Bureau *habitually* engaged in illegal surveillance, burglary, entrapment, and other similar practices under Hoover's aegis. Hoover's "resistance" to President Nixon's 1970 scheme for a coordinated "Domestic Intelligence" operation embodying some of the aforementioned practices was not based upon principle but upon both bureaucratic reservations (involving a reluctance to share "national security" jurisdiction) and a fear of exposure. The creation of the White House "Plumber's Unit," while bizarre and novel, did not diminish the *potential* of the Bureau for manipulation by an unscrupulous President or Director (indeed, nothing done by the Plumbers differed from past, and not merely occasional, Bureau practices).

Thus, Lowenthal's pioneer work eerily forecasts the role of a centralized police agency—investigating not only criminals, but "subversives" as well—which, in attenuated form, was evidenced by Watergate. Our concern is with the question of how the Bureau grew from its (not so humble) beginnings in 1908 to become both (a) a potential vehicle (as seen by Lowenthal) for a massive undermining of our Democracy and (b) a major deterrent to at least one President's ambitions to short-circuit democratic processes in conducting political warfare. In the short run, the Bureau's establishment status helped save us; in the long term, as Lowenthal's compendious tome points out, we may not be so lucky.

The following excerpt documents certain persistent themes in the Bureau's history, and all of these themes contribute to the mosaic of solid evidence that the Bureau is the preeminent component of the crime-control establishment. First of all, the Bureau is a bureaucracy which, of course, has outlasted doubting or hostile presidents, attorneys-general, and congressmen. It is a bureaucracy, moreover, which has a moral mission, a mission, to be sure, abetted by ever-increasing funding. That mission is to stamp out crime, not only federal crime, but also local crime. As Lowenthal demonstrates in his discussions of the Mann Act and local theft, the Bureau's own jurisdiction is often identical with that of state and local police forces, generally at its own insistence and, at times, against the wishes of congress. Hoover's attitudes toward "criminals" and "juvenile delinquents" have permeated law enforcement and local law enforcement elites (or, as I prefer to call them elsewhere, satellites). Although Hoover did not win every battle—his hard-line attitudes on delinquency for instance have not prevailed—no establishment in any field prevails on every issue. The question is one of reasonable consistency, and our national attitudes and local law enforcement practices have been reasonably consistent with Hoover's ideals.

Certainly, as ideologist, Hoover's beliefs about communism, anarchism, and the incipient (and, at times, overt) infiltration of movements such as the labor and civil rights activities by "subversives" contributed greatly to the unpopularity of the latter movements, at least at their inception. Lowenthal amply documents Hoover's role as guardian of public morals against both conventional criminals and subversives and his leadership in attacks against suspicious aliens as well as the International Workers of the World throughout that decade, and against American communism throughout his career. Other scholars have gone even further in analyzing Hoover's leadership—an historian of the "Red Scare" of 1919–20 has argued that Hoover (not then head of the Bureau) "exploited the whole issue of radicalism in order to enhance [the Bureau's] power and prestige."

Hoover's power over congress is also demonstrated by Lowenthal. The growth of an agency with broad investigative powers, with those famous files containing incredible amounts of damaging material (most of it unrelated to any crimes within the Bureau's jurisdiction), have ensured a muted congressional response to the Bureau's acquisition of new jurisdiction and use of controversial law enforcement techniques such as informants, *agents provocateurs,* and electronic eavesdropping. Thus in all of his roles, Hoover—as ideologist, bureaucrat, power politician, and master of congress, all abetted by a powerful public relations operation and innumerable contacts with local law enforcement agencies—was the great "establishment" figure of our times. The Watergate revelations of Spring 1973 indicate that Hoover operated independently of, often in conflict with, his nominal superiors, the President and the Attorney-General. Those revelations as well as Victor Navasky's book *Kennedy Justice,* make clear the extent of Hoover's independence and influence. His ties to business, demonstrated by the placement of many special agents (at least 4,000) into corporate enterprises and by his open partisanship in the labor wars of the '20s and '30s, also ensured the cooperation of powerful nongovernmental allies. By any definition of the term establishment, then, the Bureau, with Hoover as its sole voice for forty-eight years, clearly qualifies.

Of course, Lowenthal does not use the labels which concern us here. He does not have to; it is implicit that the Bureau is not merely another law enforcement agency. It has the capacity to make, define, and influence our criminal laws and our criminal procedures; its activities are a model for other law enforcement agencies; its missions become the missions of law enforcers, of important public groups, and, finally, of the public itself. When, as a disillusioned agent reports, Hoover opposed something—such as any softening of the criminal law's hard line toward marijuana possession in the 1967 President's Crime Commission deliberations—the unacceptable recommendation generally died a quiet death (in the instant case, however, there could be detected a slight preexpiration rattle, for the report's silence stood in stark contrast to its able staff papers pleading for marijuana decriminalization). Lowenthal has contributed greatly by documenting the Bureau's history, especially its recent history— and, as is true of the activities of the Bureau of Narcotics in 1937, history is the key to understanding the power and role of the "establishment" in contemporary political life.

The death of J. Edgar Hoover does not necessarily mean that the Bureau's importance will diminish. It acquired much of its power prior to Hoover's investiture, and momentum alone would assure retention of its vast jurisdiction. The reliance of other government agencies upon it, the continuing connections between the institution and local law enforcement, and omnipresent bureaucratic tendencies toward self-perpetuation and ever-increasing acquisition of power also ensure that the Bureau will maintain its predominant role. Indeed, the appointment of a "professional" law enforcer to replace Hoover assures that not much will change. (The victory of the Bureau's senior Bureaucrats in the fight against President Nixon's attempt to compromise both L. Patrick Gray and the Agency itself, and eventually to defeat Gray's nomination, demonstrates the F.B.I.'s continuous "staying power" as an organization which chooses to engage in "politics" only on its own terms.) Of course, Hoover's public crusades (often transformed into legal ones) against a panoply of historical and contemporary enemies may well be a thing of the past; if so (and this is by no means certain), then the rate of growth and influence may well be reduced. But, given our national preoccupations and the Bureau's central role in defining and fighting our "domestic" enemies, along with the continuing disinclination of congress to question either phenomenon, the Bureau's future seems bright.

c h a p t e r   o n e

The beginning of the crime-control bureaucracy

MAX LOWENTHAL

THE MANN ACT—THE FIRST
BIG ASSIGNMENT

The enforcement of the Mann Act began the transformation of the Justice Department's police bureau from a modest agency concerned with odds and ends of Federal law enforcement to a nationally recognized institution, with agents in every State and every large city.

The Mann Act, despite its popular purpose—the prevention of vice—had not been passed without opposition. Congressman William C. Adamson of Georgia, for example, had openly expressed his dislike of the "practice of piling up recitals of filth and iniquity . . . and then . . . running to Congress for more legislation. . . . States ought to take care of the morals . . . and not overload Congress. . . ."

The debate revolved around the evil at which the proposed law was aimed, giving little weight to the doubts expressed about the wisdom of drawing an old function of criminal law toward a central agency in Washington

The Mann Act became law; but no particular Federal detective unit was given responsibility for its enforcement. It was clear that this detective assignment might involve one of the most spectacular tasks in police history. Mr. Finch's Bureau took it.

Referring to the complaint that the Bureau of Investigation was

Abridged from *The Federal Bureau of Investigation*, by Max Lowenthal. ©
1950 by Max Lowenthal. Reprinted by permission of William Morrow & Company, Inc.

really duplicating the work which the States and localities were already doing against vice, he said that many of them were lax, and only the Bureau of Investigation would get the job done satisfactorily. Congress generally voted the requested funds in full.

The chief, now adequately financed, prepared his plans. Those plans, and their faithful execution by his detectives, were a forerunner of the nationwide dragnet methods which the Bureau of Investigation found so useful in later years.

In each city where vice was found a Department of Justice detective hired a local lawyer. The two then went to the local city police station and asked for one of the city detectives to help them. All three then went to each of the places to be investigated, and there made a census of its residents. The census was facilitated by detailed advance planning in Washington. One detail of the plan instructed the Federal detectives to ask every local police department for an order requiring the heads of the places under inquiry to cooperate with the national government. All proceeded according to plan, Mr. Finch told Congress. The city and town police "usually . . . instruct these madams . . . to . . . play fairly with the Federal Government."

In addition, the Bureau of Investigation offered to help the city police enforce their own laws. Because most violators did not cross State boundaries and therefore could not be arrested as violators of any Federal law, the Bureau urged the local police to make their own arrests for violation of local laws. The head office of the Federal detective agency studied and compiled all such laws, State by State, and gave each police agent a copy of the laws of the States.

Enforcement of the law against interstate commercial operations in vice was the only part of the Bureau's work clearly encompassed by the Mann Act. According to the Bureau's testimony in 1922, when William J. Burns was its Chief and J. Edgar Hoover its Assistant Chief, these operations had already been pretty well smashed. However, the Bureau was also arresting many persons who crossed State lines for purposes of noncommercial immorality. The principles animating the Bureau's conduct in such affairs are set forth in a treatise published by Mr. Hoover in 1938. He explained that Congress meant to attack only business transactions but actually struck at private immorality as well. The Bureau thus began to detect offenses in which "pecuniary gain," as Mr. Hoover quoted the courts, "is not an element." This was of course a far cry from what was understood by the House in 1910.

Arrests and convictions have not been limited to individual cases. Sometimes the FBI undertakes large-scale action. The principle underlying its activities in such big undertakings is to be found in an article written by Mr. Hoover in 1933. He viewed the law and its enforcers as engaged in attacking and solving what he has phrased as "the problem of vice in modern civilization."

Besides its effect in greatly augmenting the business of the FBI, the Mann Act of 1910 has had an important effect on the dossier collection of the FBI. Distressed citizens from all over the country write in to give the detectives all kinds of information about the travels of strangers, acquaintances, relatives, or even themselves. Hundreds of thousands of such communications have found their way into the swelling permanent records of the Bureau, registering and perpetuating the names, the failings (alleged or real), and the private affairs of as many victims and victimizers.

INVESTIGATION OF OPINIONS
CONTINUED

The signing of the armistice on November 11, 1918, marked the end of an era for the Bureau of Investigation. A spokesman for the Bureau had assured Congress that following the war the Bureau's budget could be cut back to peacetime levels.

Both the cutting back of the Bureau's budget and the loss of public attention by the Senate Committee were checked, however, by the appearance of a new theme—peacetime radicalism.

A solution of the jurisdictional difficulty was offered by Archibald E. Stevenson, a New York lawyer who had become an agent of the Bureau of Investigation. Mr. Stevenson's job at the Bureau was to investigate the opinions and beliefs of individuals and organizations. He first told the Committee about the wide range of pro-Germanism in this country. He said that Americans who agitated for Irish independence, such as the United Irish-American Societies and the Clan-na-Gael, were pro-German. Then he came to the point. ". . . German socialism . . . is the father of the Bolsheviki movement in Russia, and consequently the radical movement which we have in this country today has its origin in Germany."

Mr. Stevenson told of the Bureau of Investigation's raids on radical groups during the war, and of the detectives' seizure of their membership lists, their office papers, and their publications. Within ten weeks following the Armistice, radicalism seemed to have come back in full and growing strength, so that in January 1919 it had become, so he then testified, "the gravest menace to the country today."

Mr. Stevenson gave examples of radical groups and individuals agitating on the subjects of war and peace, and undermining what the American Army had accomplished on the battlefield. He condemned the secretary of the Church Peace Union for polling the clergy on conscription and conscientious objection. He spoke of the leaders of a "quasi-religious organization . . . very widespread," sentenced to twenty years in prison for advocating principles which in the opinion of the Department of Justice might hamper enlistment: this group was the International Bible Students' Association.

Mr. Stevenson then turned his testimony on the groups which wanted radical economic or political change—the Socialists, the IWW and the syndicalists, all of whom had been under the surveillance of the Bureau of Investigation. The Socialists, he told the Senators, were "a revolutionary organization . . . to undermine the rights of property and to develop class consciousness among the proletariat."

Mr. Stevenson thought they were among the most dangerous of the lot, with 250 newspapers hinting at revolution, with a "Young People's Socialist League and . . . Sunday schools" to "educate the youth in radical thinking."

As for the religious Socialist groups, they were "heathen," said Senator Nelson, and Mr. Stevenson agreed. The expert moved on to the subject of anarchism, "imported into America" from Germany. He spoke first of philosophical or "theoretical anarchism . . . opposed to violence . . . a Utopian dream." Then he described the American anarchist movement as "small . . . violent . . . pacifist. . . ."

Besides the American radicals who were said to be adopting the views of the Russian Bolshevists, other American groups received adverse mention during Mr. Stevenson's testimony. It appeared that

Bolshevism was closely related to American "reformers and pro-gressives." And besides these, there were the Americans who claimed that all, even radicals, had a Constitutional right to agitate and, when arrested, to defend themselves to the best of their ability in court. The propaganda expert told of the National Civil Liberties Bureau [now, the American Civil Liberties Union], raided by his detective associates, and of a group of clergymen, publicists, and professors who published an advertisement that confronted the Bureau of Investigation with a new danger—people's sympathy might be aroused in favor of radicals proscribed by the Bureau.

THE BOMB PLOTS

On April 28, 1919, the bureau of investigation was precipi-tated into one of the most challenging tasks it has ever undertaken —the detection of the criminals who on that date began sending bombs through the mails or by personal delivery to Government officials and to private citizens. In all, several dozen bombs were involved.

These crimes, numerous and nationwide, gave the detective force at the Department of Justice an entirely new field of operations, far different from the theoretical study of radicalism to which it had been turning its attention and in which it had helped to interest the Senate Judiciary Committee immediately after the war.

Following the 1919 bomb outrages, the task of detection was divided between two Federal detective forces. The Post Office Department's investigators were to find the bombs, while the Justice Department's agents were to find the bombers. The Post Office inspectors were able to intercept most of the bombs, so that few did any harm.

The Justice Department detectives made a prompt announce-ment of who the criminals in the 1919 cases were. The bombing jobs, they said, were the work of radicals, whose purpose was the assassination of Federal officials and the overthrow of the Govern-ment.

The theory that the bombs were sent by radicals was beset with embarrassments. The Government officials to whom the bombs were addressed included some men who were hostile to radicalism, but prominent public men whom the Bureau of Investigation sus-pected of being themselves radicals were also included.

In the course of the search, the Bureau of Investigation's men were assigned to locate and raid the homes of radicals, their families and their friends, as well as meeting halls and social settlements with radical connections. The Justice Department police holding membership in radical organizations saw to it that the dates of meetings were set by the leadership so as to suit the calendars at the Bureau's headquarters and the schedules of the raiders.

"Free rein," as the detective force reported, was given its chief. He could do whatever he thought desirable, in order to catch the bombers. The detective Bureau improvised (to quote one of its chief supporters, Congressman Martin Luther Davey of Ohio), "every conceivable method to get them with the goods." The Federal police invited the police departments of principal cities to enlist under their direction for this nationwide search. "This is the biggest job in the business of crime detection in America today," Attorney General Palmer said. The Bureau extended its operations to Canada and then called upon the police of five foreign nations to join in.

Detection of the 1918 bombing crime was at first in the hands of A. Bruce Bielaski, wartime Chief of the Bureau; he was succeeded in 1919 by Chief William J. Flynn, and in 1921 by William J. Burns. When the Bureau's anti-radical Division was created on August 1, 1919, and J. Edgar Hoover became its first Division Chief, Mr. Hoover also assumed responsibility for finding the radicals believed to have set off the bombs. His responsibility continued after 1921, when he became Assistant Bureau Chief.

Money, of course, was needed to keep the manhunt going. At all stages of the bombing investigation, from the moment it came alive and became the biggest thing in the Bureau's life, through all the later periods when the search was never permitted to lag, the detective force had to get a great deal of money. It began asking Congress for increased appropriations on June 13, 1919, eleven days after the first bombs exploded.

ATTORNEY GENERAL PALMER: ". . . Please do not cut this appropriation down, even if you think it is too big. . . . We must let these people know that we mean business."

CONGESSMAN VARE (PENNSYLVANIA): ". . . You believe that the moral effect of a large appropriation will have considerable value at this time?"

MR. PALMER: "I do. It will show these men that we are going to go the limit."

THE GID AND THE IWW

One of the major functions undertaken by the General Intelligence Division of the Bureau was the investigation of radical organizations. Attorney General Palmer described the activities as follows: "Since the first of August [1919, the date on which the GID was established] the Bureau of Investigation of this Department has been making extended investigations into the activities of the ultra-radical elements in the United States, giving particular attention to the organizations which have sponsored the feeling of unrest. . . ."

The GID gave Congress ten examples of organizations it had investigated; of these, the foremost was the Industrial Workers of the World, described by GID as "the best known of radical organizations in the United States and by far the most active and substantial so far as organization and management are concerned."

The activities stigmatized were chiefly the IWW-supported strikes. In describing the IWW strike record at length, the Federal police touched on a subject of deep concern to Congressmen from States in which the IWW were most active; those legislators were among the leaders in the movement to enact laws for the suppression of radical publications and speeches, and frequently cited the IWW organization and its strike activities as proof of the need for such laws.

The industrial relations experts of the General Intelligence Division made a study of the most important strikes in which the IWW were involved, and reminded Congress of those industrial disturbances as evidence of the revolutionary character of this organization.

During and after their wartime criminal trials the IWW claimed that they were being prosecuted for seeking correction of industrial injustices; but, the GID said in 1920, this was only a means for "inviting upon themselves a 'martyrdom' which Americanism can never justify."

As appeared from the GID reports, the detectives were always finding that when radical groups had been crushed it did not take them long to revive.

Congressmen from Pacific Coast States and from Montana, who agreed with Mr. Hoover that the IWW preached and practiced sabotage and insisted that action be taken against them, were given some hope in March 1920, when Attorney General Palmer went to Capitol Hill for more funds for the Bureau of Investigation. Mr. Palmer, seeking to explain the pressing need to Congress, mentioned the IWW and said that "in its ranks are to be found many desperate and criminal characters." However, this merely served to embarrass the GID; if crimes against the Government had been committed, the Bureau of Investigation and all its divisions, including the GID, it was suggested, ought to know of such occurrences and go out looking for the criminals.

If IWW members actually committed crimes, they did not escape for lack of attention from the Federal Bureau and the Division Chief. He and his men kept the IWW under surveillance all over the country.

WHAT THE "RED SCARE"
RAIDS ACCOMPLISHED

In June 1920 the GID, reviewing its activities in its first ten months, informed Congress that "the result of the arrests [of alien radicals] was . . . a marked cessation of revolutionary activities in the United States. For many weeks following the arrests the radical press had nearly gone out of existence in so far as its communistic tendencies were concerned. Meetings were not held of the organizations and an examination of their subsequent literature shows that they had been completely broken by the activities of the Department of Justice."

Wrecked in January, the radicals went back to work in February, the GID reported, though evidently their revival was not considered too serious as late as the middle of March, when the Attorney General went to the House Appropriations Committee and congratulated the country on the success of the Federal detectives. But, like crime, radicalism could only be checked, not effaced; therefore, despite "my long-time and well-known record for economy," the Attorney General said, the one place where Congress must not economize was in the Bureau of Investigation. Its wartime rate of expenditure must be continued after 1920, he thought, in order to safeguard the United States and to assure its survival.

Senator Walsh indicated that the raids put in question the maintenance of a general police force by the Federal Government—the objection initially made in the Sixtieth Congress to the creation of the Bureau of Investigation. He said: "In its essence the affair was an attempt to supplant the American system for the detection and punishment of crime by that in vogue in Europe."

SURVEILLANCE OVER LABOR DISPUTES

American labor unions were objects of the GID's special attention during the years 1921 to 1924. Previously, in 1919 and 1920, the GID had indicated that it was trying merely to protect conservative labor against radicals, and that the strikes it opposed were either called or instigated by the IWW or other radical organizations. This approach was broadened in the next few years and the GID took a more active part in opposing strikes of various kinds and in helping to defeat them.

THE BUREAU SURVEYS THE LEGISLATURE

Attacks on the policy and actions of the Department of Justice and the Bureau of Investigation by Senators and Congressmen led to a countermove on the part of the Bureau, which proceeded to establish espionage over the Federal legislators themselves.

Early efforts to secure an effective Congressional investigation of the Department of Justice were unsuccessful. In 1922, three Republican Congressmen introduced resolutions for the purpose, but the Republican leaders of the House turned the affair into an attack on the Department's critics. However, in the next Congress, Burton K. Wheeler of Montana, then a freshman Senator, succeeded in pushing through a resolution he had introduced to investigate the Department of Justice.

The Congressmen and Senators who made these several efforts were all added to the Bureau of Investigation's list of Congressional suspects. How many others were put under Bureau surveillance was never disclosed, although the general feeling in Congress was

that the number of the Bureau's targets among the nation's legislators was sizable.

However, full lists of the Bureau's "subjects" and full details of
its operations against members of Congress were not obtainable.
Former agents who had taken part in the espionage, or had known
about it, possessed only fragments of the full story, and employees
still at the Bureau could not afford to talk freely, even if required
by subpoena to testify.

The purpose of the Bureau's espionage was told to the Senate
Committee by a former Bureau agent who discussed the case of
Senator La Follette. At the time of the Senator's efforts to bring
about an investigation of the Teapot Dome scandal which involved
friends of the Department of Justice and the Bureau, and eventually did the greatest damage to the Administration's prestige, the
Bureau assigned agents to detect anything and everything they
could find about him, so that, as one of the resigned agents testified, "he could be stopped in what he was doing." The Bureau's
detectives investigated their subjects' lives and affairs both in their
own States and in Washington, shadowed these subjects as well
as persons who went to their Congressional offices to see them,
shadowed witnesses called before the Congressional committees
investigating official misconduct, examined the mailbags of the
legislators under surveillance, and rifled their office papers and
files.

Senator Ashurst, a member of a special investigating Committee,
summarized what it discovered: "Illegal plots, counterplots, espionage, decoys, dictographs, thousand-dollar bills, and the ex-
ploring of Senators' offices come and go in the pages of this testimony; and these devices, these plots, counterplots, spies, thousand-
dollar bills, and ubiquitous detectives were not employed . . . to
detect and prosecute crime, but were frequently employed to shield
profiteers, bribe takers, and favorites. The spying upon Senators,
the attempt to intimidate them . . . are disclosed by this record. . . ."

The investigations and criticisms, said the Department, had ul-
terior motives. The Congressional critics of the Department and
of the Bureau were assailed as benefactors, if not allies, of the
crooks and criminals whom the law-enforcing authorities were
said to be trying to convict. Attorney-General Daugherty added,
when he resigned, that among those plotting his ruin were, in

addition to lawless labor organizations, "equally powerful individuals and organizations guilty of graft upon the Government
during the World War."

The Bureau's data were assembled in support of an indictment
charging Senator Burton K. Wheeler with representation of private clients on matters coming before the Executive branch of the
Government. The Senate directed one of its committees to inquire
into the charges, and, following thorough investigation by the committee, exonerated the Senator. The jury which tried the case acquitted him.

Kenneth Crawford, Washington newspaperman, wrote subse-
quently that it was Mr. Hoover of the Bureau of Investigation
who played an active part in the affair. Paul Y. Anderson, another
Washington correspondent, writing in the Raleigh *News and Ob-
server,* said the detectives had simply concocted their story. The
Philadelphia *North American* epitomized what was generally felt
in Washington and throughout the country: "It is doubtful if there
is presented in the history of government in this country a blacker
page than this."

THE RISING TIDE OF CRITICISM

Growing opposition, from important sources, to the general
intelligence activities of the Bureau of Investigation marked the
years 1921 to 1924.

Following Mr. Daugherty's departure from the Department of
Justice at the end of March 1924, and President Coolidge's appointment of Harlan F. Stone as the new Attorney General, the Bureau
of Investigation's methods were subjected to various changes, and
its GID's anti-radical program was for the time being eliminated.

Modification of the scope of the work to be done by the Bureau
of Investigation was in effect forecast in the statement by Mr. Stone
several weeks after he took office:

"There is always the possibility that a secret police may become
a menace to free government and free institutions because it carries with it the possibility of abuses of power which are not always
quickly apprehended or understood. The enormous expansion of
Federal legislation, both civil and criminal, in recent years, however, has made a Bureau of Investigation a necessary instrument of
law enforcement. But it is important that its activities be strictly

limited to the performance of those functions for which it was created and that its agents themselves be not above the law or beyond its reach.

"The Bureau of Investigation is not concerned with political or other opinions of individuals. It is concerned only with their conduct and then only with such conduct as is forbidden by the laws of the United States. When a police system passes beyond these limits, it is dangerous to the proper administration of justice and to human liberty, which it should be our first concern to cherish. Within them it should rightly be a terror to the wrongdoer."

On October 18, 1924, two months before Mr. Hoover's title was changed from Acting Director to Director, he submitted a memorandum to his superior, Assistant Attorney General William J. Donovan, reading: "It is, of course, to be remembered that the activities of Communists and other ultra-radicals have not up to the present time constituted a violation of the Federal statutes, and consequently, the Department of Justice, theoretically, has no right to investigate such activities as there has been no violation of the Federal laws."

In 1947, Hoover published the foreword to a picture book giving the history of the FBI and said "I had no responsibility" for the 1919–1920 raids, in November 1947, when, in the course of answering a series of questions posed by the New York *Herald Tribune*, Mr. Hoover stated: "I deplored the manner in which the raids were executed then, and my position has remained unchanged."

In addition to these denials, Mr. Hoover dissociated himself from the GID in another respect. After informing Congressional Appropriations Committees of the new GID in November 1939 and in 1940, Mr. Hoover lapsed into silence on the subject; there is no reference to the GID in his subsequent annual testimony before the Appropriations Committees or in his annual reports to Congress, in the ensuing ten years.

A Senate Committee report, besides constituting a round-up of widespread feeling of the time that the FBI had, in 1939 and 1940, engaged in many illegalities suggestive of the years 1919 to 1924, served to spread that feeling in still wider circles. This was due in part to the authoritative standing of the Committee.

The Committee listed two categories of alleged wrongdoing by the police: "the recent resurgence of a spy system" over "persons

who have committed no crime, but whose economic and political
views and activities may be obnoxious to the present incumbents
of law-enforcement offices," and the employment of illegal practices
against persons accused of crime.

The illegalities committed by the police were cataloged by the
Senate Committee. The catalog reads very much like the list of
charges against the Bureau's agents in the years 1919 to 1924. An
attempt by the FBI to have its detectives inspect the information
secured by census takers in the census of 1940 only increased the
fear that it might become a central detective force with dossiers
on numberless citizens. The FBI attempt was reported in the New
York *Times* of February 27, 1940:

"The Budget Bureau disclosed today that heads of the Postal
and Treasury law enforcement agencies recently expressed dis-
approval of a request by J. Edgar Hoover, director of the Bureau
of Investigation, for legislation to permit his Bureau to inspect
the information obtained in the 1940 census.

"Their opposition was motivated in part by two factors—the
criticism which has arisen over the intimate nature of some of the
questions asked in the census and the strong opposition in some
quarters to any moves which might implement 'snooper' activities
by Federal law enforcement agencies."

The expression of fears about the FBI's constant attempts to increase its powers and about the methods it pursued became centered
to a considerable extent in the discussion of its efforts to legalize
its use of wire tapping. In 1934, Congress had declared this practice
a Federal crime, punishable by imprisonment up to two years, and
by fine in the maximum sum of $10,000. In 1937, the Supreme
Court, in the *Nardone* case, had ruled that Federal detectives were
not entitled to claim any immunity for themselves from this criminal law. Following the outbreak of World War II, the FBI asked
Congress to exempt Federal agents from this law, because "world
developments . . . have increased the gravity from the standpoint
of national safety of such offenses as espionage and sabotage."
Mr. Hoover said the FBI should be given the power to tap wires
in such cases, and also in kidnapping and extortion cases.

Mr. Hoover was taxed with the apparent contradiction between
his proposal and his prior statements that wire tapping is "unethi-
cal" and likely to make "crooks" of detectives who resort to it. The
explanation made by Mr. Hoover, and in his behalf, was that Mr.

Hoover was in reality opposed to wire tapping, but that his previous remarks should not be construed to mean anything except opposition to "uncontrolled" or "unrestricted" wire tapping.

It was claimed that abuses would be prevented by a provision in the FBI's proposal requiring the FBI to get the Attorney General's permission in each case before it could lawfully tap a wire. Chairman James Lawrence Fly of the Federal Communications Commission replied that such a provision would be meaningless. The head of the Department of Justice would not have the time to investigate the FBI's claim that it needed such authorization in cases it named, and would become, Mr. Fly said, merely a "rubber stamp."

The FBI's plea that it needed the privilege of wire tapping to detect crime efficiently was to some extent nullified by Mr. Hoover's own prior statements, recalled by Harry S Truman, then a Senator, and others, that wire tapping is ineffectual. In addition, the Senate Committee, in the report discussed above, appealed to experience that indicates that police who rely on improper and illegal methods of detection, thereby avoiding the labor involved in doing a thorough job by lawful means, "tend to defeat their own purposes; they encourage inefficiency. . . ."

Mr. Hoover's admission that he had been directing his detectives to tap wires, in the years after the Supreme Court ruled that the Federal law which made such a practice a crime applied also to Government police agencies, was coupled with various explanations. He said that the FBI's wire tapping had been carried on only "in an entirely legal manner," that it did not constitute "violation of existing laws," and that it was not done "in violation of fundamental civil rights." Two days after Mr. Hoover issued this explanation, Attorney General Jackson wrote a statement for publication, saying that "decisions of the Supreme Court . . . have in effect overruled the contentions of the Department that it might use wire tapping in its crime suppression efforts." Mr. Jackson ordered that there should be no further tapping of wires by the FBI unless and until Congress exempted it from the existing prohibitory statute. Congress has never done so.

In 1924, when the Bureau of Investigation was again under Congressional attack, Attorney General Daugherty refused to let the Committee see the confidential files relating to their alleged misconduct.

In 1931 the Bureau was again charged with improper conduct and was asked to disclose some of its secret data.

Senator Kenneth McKellar from Tennessee stated his conclusions on another occasion: "We are getting to have a tremendous secret service organization. . . . They are frequently used as a means of doing great wrong, and I have my doubts about secret service systems in a republican form of government like ours. I have been astounded at the tremendous growth and the use of large sums of money for the 'secret service,' as it is called, of the Department of Justice."

Remarks in a number of newspapers in 1940 about the great power in the Washington scene amassed by the FBI tended to raise doubt whether a resolution to investigate the Bureau, which some of them were urging, could get through either branch of Congress. Thus, the Scripps Howard newspapers published these comments: "Mr. Hoover probably has more 'powerful connections' throughout the country than any other federal bureau official. He has seen attorney generals and political machines come and go, while he has been building his FBI machine. Moreover, Mr. Hoover has had the most effective propaganda buildup of any Government employee. He is a popular hero—not only to juveniles and most of us adults with suppressed desires to be detectives, but to the simple-minded whose idea of peril to the republic is a bewhiskered plotter rather than 9,000,000 unemployed. . . . Even more formidable than Mr. Hoover, his connections and his popularity, is the national fever of fear engendered by war and depression."

Neither the Senate nor the House ordered a full-scale investigation of the FBI. Instead, the Senate adopted the resolution for an inquiry into wire tapping.

As it turned out, the inquiry took a course far different from that envisaged by the Senate Committee in its report. The subcommittee conducting the investigation ignored the record and activies of the FBI.

A President's Committee found no reason for concluding that there was anything so peculiar or unique about the FBI's operations as to justify the special status it enjoyed outside of the Civil Service System. However, before it announced this conclusion in February 1941, there had evidently been considerable tugging and pulling behind the scenes. The Washington writers specializing in news affecting Federal employees had reported from time to time on the "ticklish" problem facing the Committee and on the effort of one of its members, Supreme Court Justice Robert H. Jackson, a former Attorney General, to persuade his colleagues on the Committee to put the FBI under Civil Service.

Washington correspondents Fred Paisley and Carl Warren reported on the "undercover struggle going on before the Reed Committee on Civil Service reform." Finally, according to Washington reporters specializing in this field, a compromise was worked out in the President's Committee, to recommend that the FBI be placed under the Civil Service System, but not at that particular time. This in fact was the outcome of the Committee's work so far as the FBI was concerned.

Mr. Hoover had recommended both to Congress and to the President's Committee that his fingerprint clerks should also be exempted from Civil Service. He secured an order from the President giving the FBI this exemption, for the time being.

In the decade following these events the FBI continued to be exempt from the Civil Service System. Its detectives are still appointed in accordance with its own system.

A decade subsequent to Mr. Hoover's insistence that the Civil Service System would be ruinous to the FBI because only by being immune from that system could it secure personnel who would never break the seal of secrecy on information contained in its files, a subcommittee of the Senate Foreign Relations Committee received testimony from an FBI special agent who left it in 1945 and later entered the employ of the New York *Journal-American.* He testified that he had been providing data for publication in the Hearst press, based not only on the information he got elsewhere, but also on information he secured from another secret service agent of the FBI who had left its service in 1947—information secured by him in the course of his confidential duties.

The commercial use by ex-FBI men of information they acquired in the course of their service as special and confidential FBI agents has been increasing over the years. A number of these former agents, restricted by FBI rules from publishing any such data in books or articles while they were in its service, resigned and wrote books and articles disclosing considerable information they acquired while in FBI service. Other ex-agents have used other media of communication and dramatization.

A large and growing number of former agents have set up their own private detective and service agencies. The possible consequences of such a transfer of interests were noted even before the controversies of 1939 to 1941. In 1934, a decade after Mr. Hoover became chief of the Bureau of Investigation, a Macmillan publication, the *Encyclopedia of Social Sciences*, stated in the course of an article on private detective agencies that the heads of some of the largest private concerns "have held the highest detective jobs with the Federal Government," and presented, by way of example, the case of a former FBI man who had gone so far as to use "Government stationery on an anti-labor investigation undertaken by his agency for a private client."

Many former special agents have become advisers or heads of the labor relations departments of some of the biggest companies in the United States. Other ex-FBI agents have joined public relations and management firms doing a great deal of work for large companies in the field of labor relations—including some companies that have engaged in bitter contests with labor unions, both during the period when such FBI men were conducting its espionage over those labor unions and after the ex-agents transferred from the FBI to those companies.

In 1931 Chief Hoover informed the House Appropriations Committee that he had the "largest identification bureau in the world." The following year he amplified this: ". . . we have today practically every city and every community contributing fingerprints. We have secured this through an educational campaign showing them the advantages of this procedure."

The FBI urged every local police force, every sheriff's office, and every peace officer to fingerprint "each subject" whom they thought it "desirable to fingerprint," and then to send the print in each case to the FBI. This educational campaign continued, and before long the FBI's criminal identification file became larger by many millions than any such file anywhere in the world. The local American police forces had responded to the Bureau's educational effort by taking fingerprints of minor as well as major offenders, for transmittal to the FBI's criminal fingerprint collection. Congressman Buchanan of Texas noted in 1935 the FBI's accomplishment in this respect, referring to ". . . a sort of sentiment aroused in the country which has caused the city police, constables, deputy sheriffs, and sheriffs to take and file the fingerprints of every man they arrest, whether he is drunk or disorderly, or just fighting. . . ."

"The remarkable growth," as the FBI told all the constables and policemen of America in 1935, of the FBI's criminal identification files in Mr. Hoover's first decade as Chief had been made possible as the result of a crucial decision he reached. He rejected a rule adopted when central registries were first established in the 1890's that would have enormously reduced the potential size of the Bureau's fingerprint collection. Under this rule, promulgated in England three decades before Messrs. Burns and Hoover took up fingerprinting, the finger marks taken by the police had to be returned or destroyed in the case of persons who had been falsely arrested and had no prior criminal record.

Mr. Hoover said in 1950: "Certainly no one should have any objection to having his fingerprints taken, provided he has a clear conscience." During his first decade as Chief, Mr. Hoover officially described anyone whose prints were in the Bureau's "criminal identification" files as a person with a "criminal record." Thereafter, he revised his nomenclature, referring to such "subjects" as men and women with a "police record." In 1938 he explained the term: "A police record is a record of a man who has been arrested. It does not mean, though, that he has not later been convicted." Eight years later the FBI expanded the idea in a confidential bulletin to the local police forces of the nation: "The fingerprint files of the FBI reveal a criminal army of six million individuals who have been arrested and fingerprinted—one out of every 23 inhabitants in the United States!"

The FBI has never disclosed the total figures for the persons on whom its dossiers show a "police record," subdivided for any categories such as the following: (1) men and women convicted of no offense, major or minor; (2) strikers arrested by local police hostile to organized labor, in the decades of bitter fighting against labor union organization; (3) persons arrested for intoxication, neighborhood brawls, committing a nuisance, and the like.

Besides his "criminal" files, Mr. Hoover started, in 1933, another set of files which he has variously called "noncriminal" and "civil." He has announced his desire to include in these files the fingerprints of all persons in the United States. Although separate files are maintained for the criminal and non-criminal fingerprints, it would seem that the distinction between the two categories has not always been entirely clear. Thus, in 1941, when the FBI had the fingerprints of 23,500,000 persons in its "criminal" and "civil" dossiers, it told the press, in the course of a "round-up" of its accomplishments for national defense, that the FBI possessed "the largest reservoir of criminal records based on fingerprints in the world—more than 23,500,000 fingerprint cards."

All this has come about, in the case of the "civil" as in that of the "criminal" files, through the FBI's education of the public. That education, Mr. Hoover's testimony shows, has provided causes for semi-public organizations to take up as amateur aides to the FBI. He has listed many organizations which have voluntarily launched fingerprint campaigns to induce their own members and the general public to register with the Federal police Bureau. They "sponsor projects for fingerprinting local citizens voluntarily," Mr. Hoover explains. The way such campaigns are put on was described by the Newark (N.J.) *News* in 1941:

"Civil Identification Week [is] now being observed under sponsorship of Newark's Junior Chamber of Commerce. At the Newark booths where the general public may be fingerprinted without charge hundreds of men and women . . . [and in] some cases entire families, including small children, have presented themselves."

Magazines written for mass circulation have received material useful for articles such as the following:

"So alert to civic duty is womankind in the United States that members of many a ladies' bridge club, many a knitting club, many a sewing circle now have themselves fingerprinted in a body. . . .

"The service is absolutely free. . . .

There has been a conversion of its fingerprint collection into a base of operations—its progression from the use of the prints to check criminals for the local police, to its assumption of noncriminal identification, whether for private persons or governmental agencies; its commingling, in a detective office, of criminal business with the affairs of an increasing number of departments of American life; and its undertaking to acquire the necessary attendant skills for comprehending and performing functions related to such diverse fields as relief, military operations, and, as will now be noted, labor relations.

Among the most rewarding sources of fingerprints for the FBI dossiers have been the employment rolls of large-scale industry. The fingerprinting of employees has long been one of the subjects of agitation by some employers' associations. Evidence that this was an aim of such associations was developed in 1940 by the Senate Committee on Education and Labor, in its investigation of violation of free speech and of the rights of labor.

In January 1940, Mr. Hoover reported to the House Appropriations Committee that many industrial employers were fingerprinting their employees, and that the fingerprints were "being transmitted to the Bureau for check to ascertain whether any of these individuals have been engaged either in criminal or subversive activities."

By early 1944, the FBI has secured for its permanent dossiers the fingerprints of some thirty-seven million American workmen. This acquisition was in part due to the FBI's securing, in 1942, a directive from the War Department to all private manufacturers having contracts with that Department, requiring them to fingerprint all their employees and to send the prints to the FBI. This directive was cancelled eighteen months later.

In the meantime, despite the policy announced by Mr. Hoover in 1941 of not sending reports on fingerprints direct to employers, the FBI began at an undisclosed subsequent date to give such service to what it called "private or commercial organizations." The fact that the FBI was giving this service to private and commercial organizations which fingerprinted their employees was discussed by Mr. Hoover in February, 1947, in the course of indicating to the House Appropriations Committee that the thirty-five million dollars granted to the Bureau for the year had been insufficient; he then mentioned the fact that for lack of funds he had been obliged to discontinue his fingerprint reports to private industry.

While the published record indicated that Mr. Hoover's reports were not being made direct to employers, some disclosure had been effected, showing the types of businesses which sent the fingerprints of their employees to the FBI. Among these, besides manufacturers, were such organizations as the railroad companies and the Pullman Company. In these cases, the FBI's dealings were with the railway companies' private police forces.

NEW CRIMES TO CONQUER

The shift of the bureau's law enforcement work to local matters was accelerated after World War I.

Very soon, the Bureau's work against vice was outstripped by its work against theft. The detection of thefts has been made, under Mr. Hoover's leadership, the biggest division of the Bureau's work against criminals, providing, in peace years, from 50 to 60 per cent of the convictions in all its cases.

William D. Mitchell, President Herbert Hoover's Attorney General, said that such offenses as prostitution and auto thefts "primarily belong under State law" but that there was a "natural tendency . . . for the Federal authorities to take over those cases, and the States are willing to have them do it, because it reduces State expenses." The success of the States in this unloading operation has of course been dependent on their inducing the Bureau of Investigation to take charge of the offenses and offenders detected by the local police. This was evidently not difficult. Indeed, where the local authorities did not try to unload their work on the Federal courts and prisons, there seemed to be a need for preventing "the Federal criminal authorities from jumping in and taking over," as Attorney General Mitchell put it; he told Congress of his efforts to discourage any tendency "to grab cases away from the State criminal authorities."

One of the earliest objections to the FBI's participation in the curbing of crime already within the jurisdiction of local police forces related largely, though not exclusively, to its administration of the automobile-theft law. After this law had been in operation for eleven years, and had been used intensively by Mr. Hoover for the last five years of that period, Congressman Dyer of Missouri, the author of the law, complained that it was being used against young people who had taken cars for "joy rides . . . without any intention of committing a crime such as the one contemplated under this statute."

Shortly after the Congressman's protest, many authorities joined in urging that juvenile offenders ought not to be brought within the Federal police, court, and prison systems, and that they ought to be dealt with in their own home communities. This was the view expressed by the Wickersham Commission, established by President Herbert Hoover in 1929 for the study of improved procedure in dealing with criminals, by Attorney General Mitchell, by the Federal Bureau of Prisons, and by the Children's Bureau of the Labor Department.

Despite the general agreement on this point, the Bureau of Investigation has administered the automobile-theft law in such a way as to bring into the Federal court and prison system large numbers of juvenile "joy riders," so that since 1946 juveniles violating that statute have constituted more than half of all the juvenile delin-quents brought into the Federal system and imprisoned in Federal institutions.

JURISDICTIONAL PROBLEMS

The enactment of new Federal laws giving the FBI most of its criminal business results from two major causes. One was men-tioned by Attorney General Mitchell in 1932; he referred then to the indignation aroused when a particularly heinous crime has been committed. At such a time there is a general feeling that something should be done about crime, and some legislators and others say that there ought to be a law for the purpose. Since there are already State criminal laws covering the subject matter, the cry is for an-other law, this time a Federal criminal statute.

A second factor producing Federal statutes which duplicate State criminal laws is the feeling that by such means the effectiveness of organized society against wrongdoers is increased. This feeling in part arises out of the belief that if the number of police forces de-tecting any category of crime is increased, the perpetrator of that type of crime will realize that he will be more readily detected and will be more inclined to be discouraged from criminal activity. The feeling that the creation of Federal jurisdiction over crime, along-side the local jurisdiction, will discourage criminals has also been due to the belief, stimulated by Mr. Hoover, that some local police forces are inefficient and "publicity-mad," and that the entrance of the FBI into any crime detection work will eventually introduce efficiency as well as restraint in the proceedings.

The theory that, when police agencies have duplicate or concur-rent jurisdiction, criminals will be discouraged, and the belief that the FBI is far more efficient than local police forces, have been at the bottom of the constant efforts of various business associations to secure Federal laws expanding the FBI's jurisdiction. The drive by the officials of such associations was discussed in the House by Con-gressman Celler, in the course of his defense of the FBI in 1940: ". . . You all know of the efforts of various groups of businessmen to secure various types of legislation to protect their interests and of their demands upon Members of Congress to pass legislation which will enable the Federal Bureau of Investigation to extend the scope of its activities into their fields of operation in order that they may receive the protection which this Bureau obviously affords."

Efforts of this nature by business concerns have been the subject of plain-spoken as well as of carefully guarded objections by Federal officials. Attorney General Mitchell two decades ago, and, recently, the Director of the Federal Bureau of Prisons, have touched on the adverse consequences of such attempts by business concerns. It has required courage to voice objections to business proposals for increasing FBI jurisdiction. Attorney General Mitchell told Congress in 1932 that when he opposed the efforts to give the FBI its jurisdiction—since conferred—over the "interstate" theft of merchandise, "I was roundly abused by insurance companies and other people for standing in the way of enforcement of law and detection of criminals."

With some of the business associations, some of the Federal legislators, and the FBI agreeing that its participation in crime work makes crime detection more efficient and that its dread name discourages criminals from continuing in their way of life, the only remaining question is whether criminals believe what these authorities state. Apparently they do not. As already noted, in the area of the FBI's largest activity, the theft of automobiles, there has been no substantial diminution of crime during the twenty-six years of Mr. Hoover's management of the Bureau and of his campaign against automobile thieves.

The problem of waste involved in a duplication of Federal and local police forces for the handling of the same kind of law enforcement, and the additional financial burden on the Federal government, have come up for discussion from time to time in the twenty-six years since Mr. Hoover became head of the Bureau. In 1932, Attorney General Mitchell said to the House Appropriations Committee: "We talk about economy and about reducing Federal bureaus and Federal expense and all that, and in the next breath we talk about projecting the Central Government into handling the crime situation. . . ."

Four years later, Senator McKellar spoke to Chief Hoover about the increase in the annual expenditure of his bureau from $2,250,000 in 1928 to $4,380,000 in 1935.

SENATOR MCKELLAR: ". . . Do you not think we ought to reduce the amount that we have allowed you? . . .

"Now, in 1936, you ask for $5,000,000, which is almost double what you spent in 1934, and a tremendous increase over the Budget estimate of 1935. . . . It seems to me your Department is just running wild, Mr. Hoover."

CHIEF HOOVER: "May I point this out, Senator? There were a series of crime bills—the kidnapping statute, the extortion statute, the bank-robbery statute, the fugitive law, the stolen-property law, and several others enacted by Congress, which have greatly increased our work."

INVESTIGATION OF BELIEFS

In 1924 Mr. Hoover noted that "theoretically" the Bureau of Investigation "has no right to investigate" non-criminal activities. By 1940 he had reached the conclusion that the FBI's jurisdiction included the right to investigate "subversive activities" and persons engaged "in any subversive activity or in movements detrimental to the internal security." The FBI had already illustrated, in 1935, its concept of the scope of such terms as "subversive," when Mr. Hoover condemned, as guilty of "subversive acts," those "convict lovers" who favor what Mr. Hoover regards as abuses of parole. Further indication was given, in 1938, of FBI concepts in this general area; at that time, in listing the different categories of cases within its jurisdiction, the FBI included "strikes" in the same category as "treason."

Considerable opposition to the FBI's re-entrance into the non-criminal field was voiced in many quarters in 1940. *Railroad Train-man,* official journal of the Brotherhood of Railroad Trainmen, said:

"Hoover is now engaged in a nation-wide search of those whom he considers are indulging in 'subversive activities.' [To] Hoover . . . 'subversive activities' are apt to be any activities or opinions which he dislikes, and that includes the legitimate and lawful activities of organized labor. The FBI has been investigating the employ-ees of many factories 'to ascertain whether any of those individuals have been engaged in subversive activities.' Congress has not author-ized Hoover to use Government money to operate an OGPU and spy upon men engaged in non-criminal activities which J. Edgar Hoover dislikes. In his activities following the World War [I], Hoover compiled a list of half a million persons . . . he regarded as possessing economic or political beliefs or engaging in activities amounting to what he considered 'ultra-radicalism.' The equivalent

of one person out of every sixty families in America was on his
shameful spy list. . . ."

From time to time, Mr. Hoover has indicated how the FBI gets
the names of persons whom it investigates on charges that they are
"subversive." In September 1939 he called for the assistance of the
general public, and in particular wrote to "banks, business houses
[and] railroads" soliciting their help. Mr. Hoover and his branch
chiefs called in "for conference the officials of the various plants"
employing labor on national defense contracts. The FBI told them
of its program for protecting their plants. By November 1939 Mr.
Hoover was able to report that the employers had been giving him
"excellent cooperation." The extent and possibly the nature of the
FBI's relationship with private concerns and banks influential all
over the United States is indicated by Mr. Hoover's testimony at the
beginning of 1940 that "we have jurisdiction over 19,240 banks. . . .
We have carried on a very intensive and extensive educational campaign in the banks under the provisions of the Federal statutes. . . ."

The result of the FBI's campaign has been the investigation of
hundreds of thousands, if not millions, of complaints by individuals
against other persons. Early in the past decade, Mr. Hoover said
that almost all such complaints have substance—a view quite different from that expressed by Attorney General Gregory during the
World War I period when he said that most of the complaints sent
in were sheer nonsense.

In addition to building up FBI dossiers on persons attacked by
neighbors or acquaintances as "subversive," the FBI has retained a
vast number of other names mentioned incidentally in the complaints or acquired by its detectives in investigating the charges it
receives. Once a name is brought into an inquiry, by whatever
means, it becomes part of the FBI's permanent records, and information or charges against the person thus included or mentioned in
any investigation acquire the permanent status of "information . . .
maintained in the files."

The FBI's role in investigating the two million Federal employees
whose selection is not subject to confirmation by the Senate has
raised other problems besides that of the advisability of its participation in this work. One of these problems, a subject of continuing
and still unresolved discussion, relates to the question of whether
the FBI's undercover operatives shall be subject to cross-examina-

tion by employees they accuse of disloyalty. Mr. Hoover opposed any disclosure of informants' names in the loyalty board hearings. The FBI said that, if it disclosed the names of its informers, they would no longer be useful to the Bureau, as they would be unable to continue their undercover membership in "subversive" organizations. Similarly, the FBI took the position that it could not disclose the names of any informants such as neighbors, acquaintances or fellow employees without their specific consent, lest other potential informants be deterred by the prospect of having their identities known.

The type of data collected by the FBI's agents, transmitted to headquarters, and included in summarized reports prepared for the FBI's higher-ups, was disclosed at the Coplon trial in Washington, D.C., in June 1949. The disclosure was not made until after the Federal prosecutor, as the press reported, "pleaded with judge Albert L. Reeves not to place the top-secret FBI report 'before the world' lest the Nation's security be imperiled." When the Judge ruled against him, the Government prosecutor asked that various of the FBI documents be disclosed only to the jury. The Washington *Post* reported the judge's ruling: "Courts of law are open to the public. I have no right to say to newspapermen or the public that they can't be here—they have a right to be here."

When the documents were disclosed in the courtroom, the public and press had an opportunity to learn what kind of material the FBI was guarding in its files as top-secret and also the nature of the data it was amassing about individuals on whom it maintained files. One example of the documents that came to light was a confidential report of an FBI agent who had been told by an informant what he in turn had been told by his young son—namely, that the child had seen their neighbor going about undressed while in his own home.

An illustration of what the FBI classified as top-secret was the report of an FBI undercover operative telling of an advertising throwaway he had picked up from a New York City sidewalk. He included as confidential data the names of the prospective public speakers at a meeting in Madison Square Garden.

The New York *Times* reviewed the incident and its aftermath as follows: "The Federal Bureau of Investigation, which has enjoyed an immunity from high-level criticism almost unparalleled among Government agencies, found itself this week in a state of acute embarrassment as a result of public disclosure of some of its investigative techniques.

"Now, for the first time in history, a group of these dossiers containing unsupported and unevaluated tips from anonymous 'confidential informants,' along with the documented, eye-witness reports of FBI agents themselves, have been laid out for public inspection. . . ."

Some six weeks after the storm broke, Mr. Hoover presented his own statement, in the FBI's Law Enforcement Bulletin. The United Press published this summary of Mr. Hoover's remarks:

"J. Edgar Hoover, director of the Federal Bureau of Investigation, today struck back at critics of his agency, accusing them of 'politics,' 'selfishness' and 'wanton disregard for the truth.' . . .

"He said it was 'inexcusable' to criticise a law enforcement agency when the attacks were 'not based on facts. . . .' "

Defense of the Bureau's newly revealed practices by other supporters as well as by Mr. Hoover raises an issue similar to the one that caused such a furor in the Sixtieth Congress, some forty years ago, and ten years thereafter in the Senate Judiciary Committee investigation. The Bureau's defenders maintain that the accumulation of such miscellaneous data in the FBI's files is justifiable on the ground that it may come in handy some time in the future even if its immediate relevance is not established. This policy is the realization of the fear expressed during the Sixtieth Congress. That fear, it will be recalled, was that the newly established Federal police force at the Department of Justice might some day adopt practices habitual to political police systems in Europe but abhorrent to a democracy. Among these practices noted in the Congressional discussions of 1908–1909 are the collection and lodgment in police files of rumors, suspicions and gossip, as well as data about the private life of every non-criminal placed under police surveillance.

It was against the growth of such practices that fears were expressed and protests made in 1919, when the Bureau of Investigation aided in the collection and filing of large quantities of material of this nature.

II
The beginning and growth of the drug-control establishment

The prime competitor for the F.B.I.'s mantle of leadership within the crime-control establishment, and a prime shaper of contemporary attitudes about crime, is the Drug Enforcement Administration (formerly the Bureau of Narcotics). Although a public controversy rages about decriminalizing simple possession of marijuana, few know of the critical role of this member of the crime-control establishment in fostering and perpetuating myths about drugs, both soft and hard. The notion that drug "abuse" is a proper subject for the criminal law—and that such law and its procedures are effective in combatting such abuse—is now widespread. It is intriguing to learn, as Dr. Alfred Lindesmith informs us in the excerpt from his book *The Addict and the Law,* that our attitudes toward this critical social problem were engendered not by medical findings or by public outrage, but by the activities of the Bureau of Narcotics, formerly located in the Treasury Department and later housed (under the title of Bureau of Narcotics and Dangerous Drugs) in the Justice Department.

Like Hoover, Harry Anslinger, the Bureau's first Director, carried on a moral crusade. In doing so, he sponsored federal legislation, encouraged state efforts, endorsed dubious "scientific findings" about drug abuse, and disparaged those who disagreed with his findings. Indeed, in the relatively narrow area of drugs, he was even more influential than was Hoover in his broader domain. Anslinger and his agency in effect created the drug scare, rather than merely exploiting it. Since drugs and crime have become popularly equated, Anslinger's views have had an even profounder impact upon the public than he might at first have foreseen.

Lindesmith chillingly details the variety of methods used to create and perpetuate that scare. Indeed, narcotics abuse and narcotics-related crimes have increased (perhaps not as dramatically as the mass media would have us believe, but certainly significantly) largely because the law has actively intervened to distort what are essentially medical problems. Addicts are not seen as sick or their addiction pathological; they are criminals. Since the crime is a consensual one with no victim, police must actively participate in discovering—or, as we know, in creating—it. Again, like the FBI, an ostensible law enforcement agency has become a public crusader; its views are accepted and acted upon by congress and the state legislatures; its "expertise" is utilized to create new crimes and new crime waves.

The historical background of the Bureau's activities is, of course, highly relevant to our contemporary drug problems, for the history is a continuing one. Today, only marijuana criminalization (also largely the creation of the Bureau, as Arthur Millspaugh's dispassionate analysis points out) is a matter of public inquiry. Lindesmith's analysis of the Bureau of Narcotics' role in relation to heroin clearly demonstrates that that problem should be of equal concern to those wishing to confine the criminal law to its proper sphere. The activities of the Bureau—its ability to coöpt the medical profession and Congress—indicate that this most powerful segment of the establishment will retain its pervasive—and deleterious—influence.

The passage of the Marijuana Tax Act of 1937—feared by Millspaugh—only enhanced the authority of the Bureau in the eyes of the public and its influence upon other sectors of law enforcement. Today, its beliefs and precepts command virtually universal acceptance—with the possible single exception of marijuana possession—and we no longer even bother to ask the truly fundamental questions raised by Lindesmith. In addition to sponsoring marijuana legislation, the Bureau has used precisely the techniques it applied so well to its antiheroin crusade to convince the public of marijuana's danger and of the perfidy of reform advocates.

One possible reason underlying Anslinger's anti-marijuana "crusade" is analyzed in the article by Donald T. Dickson. His perspective is unique and interesting: the crusade against marijuana was undertaken largely to maintain the viability and integrity (physical, that is) of the Bureau itself. The reason for the crusade may well have been functional—the need to maintain congressional funding, with its symbolic overtones of power and influence. The article demonstrates the dilemma faced by all law enforcement agencies—they must simultaneously argue that their work is effective (*e.g.* that crime has been reduced) but that more money is needed to wage the war. Anslinger's answer, as well as Hoover's, was simply to find new dangers to combat (while claiming victory—though never complete victory—over the old ones). This study does not refute, it should be noted, the possibility that Anslinger may well have had mixed motives for undertaking his crusade.

Dickson also casts valuable, though indirect, light on our comprehension of establishments. An "establishment" is most likely to be located in a relatively permanent group (or combination of groups) rather than in, let us say, Congress or other elected bodies subject to the stresses and vagaries of politics. With the increasing bureaucratization of many governmental functions, oversight by Congress tends to drop. Crusades by bureaucracies wielding potent weapons of "scientific expertise" will rarely be questioned by Congress—indeed, funding will increase. Also, the ability of a Federal bureaucratic "crime-fighting" organization to influence its state compatriots is obviously more substantial than the reverse. The Federal agencies are generously funded, operate in every state, and are imbued with the aura of "professionalism" often so critical to acceptance of controversial "crime-fighting" plans. A Federal bureaucracy is also much more likely to generate publicity than is a state agency—especially publicity on a national level. Most of the publicity will, of course, tend to make legitimate, to the public, the activities of that agency.

c h a p t e r t w o

The politics of drug-control:
its early history

ARTHUR MILLSPAUGH

It was found in 1909 that the United States was importing 200,000 pounds of opium a year, while our legitimate medical requirements were only 50,000. Thereupon, Congress prohibited the importation of opium and its preparations and derivatives except for medicinal use.

At about the same time, a meeting of the International Opium Commission at Shanghai inaugurated a series of international conferences and agreements, each of which has had a significant relationship to the development of our domestic legislation and administration. The Hague Opium Conference of 1912 formulated a Convention for the Suppression of the Abuse of Opium and Other Drugs, whereby each power promised to "enact efficacious laws or regulations for the control of the production and distribution of raw opium."

To carry out the provisions of this Convention, Congress enacted two laws in 1914. One regulated the importation of opium, prohibited the exportation of smoking opium, and permitted the export of opium and cocaine and their derivatives only to countries regulating their entry. The second law repealed those portions of the act of 1890 which related to smoking opium produced in the United States, increased the internal revenue tax to $300, and laid down certain requirements for obtaining a license to manufacture. Congress on December 17, 1914 passed what is familiarly known as

Abridged from pp. 80–83, 286–87 of *Federal Crime Control,* by Arthur Millspaugh (Washington, D.C.: The Brookings Institution, 1937). © 1937 by The Brookings Institution. Reprinted by permission of the publisher.

the "Harrison Narcotic Law," which provided for the registration of dealers in narcotic drugs and aimed to restrict the business to persons so registered. The act of January 17, 1914 has also been amended. It was provided, for example, in 1924, that no crude opium might be imported for the purpose of manufacturing heroin.

The United States Senate, on March 31, 1932, advised and consented to the ratification of the Convention for Limiting the Manufacture and Regulating the Distribution of Narcotic Drugs (known as the Narcotic Limitation Convention of 1931), and the formal instrument of ratification was transmitted, under the terms of the Convention, on April 10, 1932. This Convention came into force July 9, 1933, and considerably tightened both international supervision and domestic control, the intention being to limit manufacture in all manufacturing countries to the medicinal requirements of the world. Administratively, this control involves (1) determination of medicinal requirements, (2) control of imports, (3) internal revenue collections, (4) licensing and registration of manufacturers and dealers, and (5) detection, apprehension, and punishment of illicit importers, manufacturers, and dealers.

From other angles, Congress has attacked the drug evil. An act of January 19, 1929 provided for the establishment of two federal institutions for the confinement and treatment of persons addicted to the use of habit-forming narcotic drugs.

The problem of organizing narcotics control has not been a simple one. At first, in March 1915, a Narcotic Section was created in the Miscellaneous Division of the Bureau of Internal Revenue to enforce the Harrison Narcotic Law, the necessary field investigative work being performed by internal revenue agents as a part of their duty in enforcing general internal revenue laws. Narcotic-law enforcement was transferred in January 1920 to a Narcotic Division organized in the newly created Prohibition Unit of the Bureau of Internal Revenue. Field investigative work was then performed by narcotic agents and inspectors under the supervision of prohibition agents. In July 1921, however, narcotic field-enforcement districts were established under the supervision of narcotic agents who reported directly to the Prohibition Unit, thus constituting a field enforcement organization, separate from that established for prohibition. On April 1, 1927, the Bureau of Prohibition was created in the Treasury Department, under which narcotic-law enforcement was delegated to the Narcotic Unit in charge of a Deputy Commissioner of Prohibition. The special force of narcotic agents and inspectors remained in the field and reported to the Prohibition Bureau (Narcotic Unit). Under the act of June 14, 1930, the federal Narcotics Control Board was abolished and the present Bureau of Narcotics established in the Treasury Department. The Narcotics Limitation Convention of 1931 requires each of the contracting powers to "create a special administration" for the purpose of carrying out the provisions of the Convention. While "special administration" does not mean "independent agency," the United States is obligated to assign narcotics enforcement to some special bureau, section, or unit devoted exclusively to that function.

During the appropriation hearings in December 1934, the Commissioner of Narcotics explained that, if an attempt were made by the federal government to control marihuana, "You would have to put a tax on corn plasters and medicines containing it." But, he added,

. . . the way to control that drug, as I told the chiefs of police at this crime conference, is to go back home and have a city ordinance enacted.[1] We get requests from chiefs of police all over the country, after raiding criminal hideouts and finding marihuana, asking us what to do about it. We tell them, "Your city council can enact an ordinance overnight to make unlawful cultivation, possession, and sale."

Down in Florida they had a horrible tragedy. A young boy who used the drug killed his whole family. Public opinion was aroused. They passed a uniform narcotic drug act. . . . The state has the power. They have been making headway in Florida and California against the marihuana peddler.[2]

The Commissioner went on to explain that marihuana could not be controlled by the federal government through the interstate commerce clause, since there is practically no interstate commerce in the drug. Stating that he would not recommend federal regulation of this substance, he was asked if his opposition "was due to the fact that it would take a larger force to enforce it." He replied:

Oh, no, sir; not that. It is a question of having the states say, "All right, Uncle Sam is doing it."

[1] The same, pp. 354–55.
[2] 74 Cong. 1 sess., *Treasury Department Appropriation Bill for 1936*, Hearings before H. Committee on Appropriations, p. 210.

I am putting a marihuana provision, included in the proposed uniform state narcotic drug law before every legislature next month, to enact. If the states will go along with that, then the federal government ought to step in and co-ordinate the work, but until the states become conscious of their own problem I think it is a mistake for the federal government to take on the whole job.[3]

Two years later, the Commissioner testified:

The states have certainly gone to work on this law. We have now only the District of Columbia, Tennessee, and South Carolina that do not have marihuana legislation.[4]

Nevertheless, a bill was drafted in the Treasury Department and introduced in the 1937 session of Congress to suppress the marihuana evil through the federal taxing power. If it passes, Uncle Sam once more will be "doing it."

The tendency is now, as we have seen, to define the jurisdictions of federal law-enforcement agencies largely through applications of the interstate commerce, taxing, and postal clauses of the Constitution. With reference to general crimes, which make up increasingly the jurisdiction of the Bureau of Investigation, reliance is chiefly on the interstate commerce clause. The result is a multiplying of concurrent jurisdictions and of overlapping operations. Is this result in the long-run desirable?

State and local administration, it would seem, can be strengthened, without extending federal jurisdiction, by centralizing law enforcement *within* the states through the creation of state police departments and allocating to such departments the criminal-law enforcement functions of the counties and municipalities, except possibly a few of the most populous ones.

3 The same, p. 211.
4 75 Cong. 1 sess., *Treasury Department Appropriation Bill for 1938*, Hearings before H. Committee on Appropriations, p. 184.

c h a p t e r   t h r e e

The drug-control bureaucracy creates the "drug problem"

ALFRED LINDESMITH

"With the language of this law we can trap addicts like animals."
—COMMENT BY AN OFFICIAL

ADDICTION AND THE LAW

The present program of handling the drug problem in the United States is, from the legal viewpoint, a remarkable one in that it was not established by legislative enactment or by court interpretations of such enactments. Public opinion and medical opinion had next to nothing to do with it. It is a program which, to all intents and purposes, was established by the decisions of administrative officials of the Treasury Department of the United States. After the crucial decisions had been made, public and medical support was sought and in large measure obtained for what was already an accomplished fact.

Another unusual feature of the federal narcotic laws is that, while they are in legal theory revenue measures, they contain penalty provisions that are among the harshest and most inflexible in our legal code.

The basic antinarcotic statute in the United States is the Harrison Act of 1914. It was passed as a revenue measure and made abso-

Abridged from pp. 3–5, 8–10, 16–18, 20, 27–28, 33–34, 54–56, 163–64, 170–73, 243–45, 247–49, 262, 266, 276 of *The Addict and the Law*, by Alfred Lindesmith (Bloomington: Indiana University Press, 1965). Reprinted by permission of the publisher.

lutely no direct mention of addicts or addiction. Its ostensible purpose appeared to be simply to make the entire process of drug distribution within the country a matter of record. There is no indication of a legislative intention to deny addicts access to legal drugs or to interfere in any way with medical practices in this area. Thus, the act provided that:

Nothing contained in this section shall apply: (a) to the dispensing or distribution of any of the aforesaid drugs to a patient by a physician, dentist, or veterinary surgeon registered under this Act in the course of his professional practice only.

There were two major influences which led to the enactment of federal narcotic legislation at that time. One of these was that American representatives to international conferences had, before 1914 (e.g., at The Hague Convention in 1912), urged other governments to establish systems for the internal control of narcotic drugs. It was therefore inconsistent that the United States itself did not have such a system. The other influence developed from a growing realization that there were relatively large numbers of addicts in the United States and an impression that the problems posed by this fact were not being effectively met by the various measures adopted by different states and localities.

EARLY INTERPRETATION OF THE ACT

The passing of the Harrison Act in 1914 left the status of the addict almost completely indeterminate. The Act did not make addiction illegal and it neither authorized nor forbade doctors to prescribe drugs regularly for addicts. Yet, within a few years regular administration of drugs to addicts was declared to be legal only in the case of aged and infirm addicts in whom withdrawal might cause death and in the case of persons afflicted with such diseases as incurable cancer. Current regulations of the Federal Bureau of Narcotics are still substantially the same with respect to these points.

THE LINDER CASE (1925)

Reiterating that the Harrison law was a revenue measure, the Court added the following important statement:

It [the act] says nothing of "addicts" and does not undertake to prescribe methods for their medical treatment. They are diseased and proper subjects for such treatment, and we cannot possibly conclude that a physician acted improperly or unwisely or for other than medical purposes solely because he has dispensed to one of them, in the ordinary course and in good faith, four small tablets of morphine or cocaine for relief of conditions incident to addiction. What constitutes bona fide medical practice must be determined upon consideration of evidence and attending circumstances.

The two new elements in this decision are (a) the Court's explicit espousal of the view that addiction is a disease and (b) the rule that a physician acting in good faith and according to fair medical standards may give an addict moderate amounts of drugs to relieve withdrawal distress without necessarily violating the law.

The question of what constitutes proper medical care is a medical issue and therefore, presumably, one to be settled, not by legislators, judges, juries, or policemen, but by the medical profession. The present punitive system of dealing with addicts and the Treasury Department regulations on which it is based are in direct violation of federal law and based upon an unconstitutional interpretation of the Harrison Act.

The reason for the lack of distinction in the statutes between addict and peddler again represents a sacrifice of principle for expediency. The original formulation in 1915 of the theory that mere possession of illicit drugs by an addict was an offense may well have reflected pressure from enforcement sources, which have always complained of the difficulty involved in proving sale. The possession doctrine makes it easier to convict peddlers, and even easier to convict addicts. Placing the victim of the peddler under the same penalties as those provided for peddlers serves another extremely vital enforcement function by providing the leverage to force addicts to cooperate with the police in trapping higher sources of supply. All of this makes sense from the enforcement viewpoint, but it does not make sense if the addict is viewed as a diseased person, for it subjects him to exploitation not only by peddlers but also by the police.

The narcotics statutes are characterized by harshness and inflexibility of penalties and by the extraordinary limitations placed upon judicial power to mitigate sentences in accordance with circumstances surrounding individual cases or to place certain persons on probation rather than sending them to prison. They have aroused opposition from judges and from many other sources. The power to mitigate punishment, which was taken out of the hands of the judges, was not simply eliminated by these laws as one might suppose from merely reading them; it was rather transferred to the police and prosecutors. The latter can now virtually fix sentences in most instances by manipulating the charge and recommending sentences to the court, and they can grant probation in the same way. Since the laws were virtually written by police and prosecution interests, it is not surprising that this should be so, for laws of this sort give police and prosecutors greater freedom in making deals with offenders and permit them to punish defendants who refuse to cooperate with a minimum of judicial interference. The serious question which is raised, however, is whether the administration of justice ought to be placed so completely in the hands of prosecution interests.

When the Boggs Act was passed in 1951 many of the states passed "Little Boggs Laws" of their own, just as they later imitated the 1956 legislation. Suspension of sentence and probation were barred.

NONFEDERAL LEGISLATIVE TRENDS

Before about 1930 drug offenses were generally regarded as a matter of federal concern and very few of the states had adequate laws or did a great deal in this field. When the Federal Narcotics Bureau was created in 1930 it at once set about securing greater cooperation from the states and tightening up the legal situation by urging upon them the enactment of a Uniform Narcotics Law which was prepared between 1927 and 1932. This law, modeled after the federal statutes, was designed to facilitate enforcement by promoting cooperation between federal and nonfederal officers, by creating uniform standards of record-keeping on state and federal levels, and by eliminating certain gaps in the provisions of the federal laws occasioned by constitutional limitations upon the police powers of the national government.

The Uniform Narcotics Act has been adopted by most of the states although the penalty provisions, left blank in the recommended Act, vary from state to state. As penalties were increased by the 1951 and 1956 national legislation, the states have quickly followed suit and in many instances enacted even harsher penalties.

In 1951 the Congress enacted the Boggs Bill, which sharply increased penalties for narcotics offenders. It also greatly enlarged the budget of the Federal Narcotics Bureau, authorized the employment of more agents, and provided more money to be used to purchase illicit drugs as evidence. Public concern over juvenile addiction was at a fever pitch at that time and the police were being blamed for it by some. Federal narcotics officials had generally discounted this problem, arguing that the extent of such addiction was being greatly exaggerated. Nevertheless, the drive was said to have been aimed at this teen-age problem. It thus served, not only to justify the Narcotics Bureau in the eyes of Congress, but also to appease and quiet a worried public.

Informed public opinion in this country is now fully aware of the fact that Britain, and most other European and Western nations, permit their addicts access to legal drugs and that none of these nations has a drug problem that represents more than a tiny fraction of the problem in the United States.

At the White House Conference on addiction in September 1962 very little attention was given to any foreign programs. Professor Edwin M. Schur, who had just published what may fairly be described as a definitive study of British practices on the basis of two years of on-the-spot observation and inquiry, was allotted two minutes at the very end of one session. Earlier in the session another speaker had, in a much longer speech, told the audience that the British program was essentially the same as the American. No attention at all was devoted to any of the many other successful foreign programs. The President's Ad Hoc Committee which met before the 1962 White House Conference, as well as the President's Advisory Commission appointed after the conference, which issued its report in November 1963 gave little attention to foreign experience or dismissed it as irrelevant.

OFFICIAL VS. PUBLIC OPINION

For a considerable number of years after 1954 the Federal Bureau of Narcotics circulated an anonymous, undated document attacking the present writer and seeking to discredit the British program or deny its existence. This document opened as follows:

> Several years ago a professor of sociology at an American university who is a *self-appointed expert* on drug addiction, after interviewing a few drug addicts, wrote an article in which he advocated that the United States adopt the British system of handling drug addicts by having doctors write prescriptions for addicts. "Adopt the British system" is now urged by *all self-appointed narcotic experts who conceal their ignorance of the problem*

by ostentation of seeming wisdom. The statement was recently used by a Columbia University professor on a television program and in a national press release in advocating this system. A Citizen's Advisory Committee report to the Attorney General of California urged the British system. It has appeared in articles by university professors in several states. The Yale University Law Review published a supporting article. It is now accepted as a fact. [Italics added.]

Nothing could be further from the truth. The British system is the same as the United States system. . . .

This states the theme which the Bureau of Narcotics and its followers have been promoting during the last decade. It is a theme which the new head of the Bureau, Henry L. Giordano, has taken over from his predecessor.

The tactics followed by the Bureau under Mr. Anslinger were, in the main, to deny that the British program is any different from ours, to equate the program with the clinic system, to disparage the accuracy and reliability of British official reports and statistics, to include Hong Kong in Britain, and to argue that the British program is not a "system."

From an interview by Pete Martin with the new head of the Federal Bureau of Narcotics reported in the *American Legion Magazine,* it is apparent that the Bureau is continuing to stick to its guns. The following conversation is reported:

MARTIN: I'd like to begin by asking you about the difference between the American system and the English system of narcotics control. I understand that in England they have free clinics for addicts to get their daily shot; while in this country we discarded that system back in the twenties and are more inclined to grab the addicts and institutionalize them.

GIORDANO: The so-called British system has been discussed many times in this country—and tried as you mentioned—but there's really very little difference between the methods actually practiced today in England and those employed here. Dr. Granville Larimore and Dr. Henry Brill from New York State went over there to study British methods. . . . When they came back they said in effect that they could find very little difference between the control method used in England and here. . . .

Britain has never made a real census of drug addiction. For three years they've published figures, indicating they had 350 addicts, two years ago 400, and last year 500. This seems unrealistic when not long ago they tried and convicted a doctor for selling drugs to hundreds of addicts among his "patients" alone! The only figures they have in the United Kingdom are when a doctor chooses to report them.

MARTIN: Five hundred seems a completely unrealistic figure to me. Just what is this British system?

GIORDANO: As far as we're concerned, there really isn't such a thing, even though everyone talks as if there is. The trouble is they seem to have ignored the problem, apparently have refused to acknowledge it. Now in Hong Kong, where they have an accurate census, they admit having 200,000 to 250,000 addicts, and it is a serious, sizable problem. The British have a growing marijuana problem at home, too.

There are a number of puzzling aspects in the above remarks. For example, if the British program is no different from ours, what does Mr. Giordano mean by agreeing with Martin that the program was tried in this country in the 1920's and abandoned? Also, if the programs are the same, why try to show that the program in England is not as effective as claimed? Giodano's reference to an English doctor who sold drugs to his patients seems to be a reference to Dr. John Bodkin Adams. Dr. Adams, however, was tried for murder, not for selling drugs, and he was acquitted.

Narcotics enforcement officials at the state and municipal levels generally follow the line established by the Federal Bureau of Narcotics and if they read any of the literature it is most likely to be materials distributed by the Bureau.

OBSTACLES TO REFORM

In an editorial entitled "Dismantling a Narcotic Theory," the *Wall Street Journal* early in 1964 commented favorably on the recommendation of the President's Advisory Commission that the Federal Bureau of Narcotics be eliminated in its present form and that its functions be turned over to other agencies. The Bureau, said the editorial, "has become a symbol of a single theory of dealing with drug addiction. This theory rests on the premise that addiction is a crime and, for all practical purposes, little more than that." Observing that this theory has been followed by the government for nearly half a century, the *Wall Street Journal* suggests that it be dismantled along with the Bureau of Narcotics. As presently organized the Bureau depends for its very existence upon the status quo, and it is therefore easy to understand that it has come to be the symbol of a punitive approach and the most important and influential obstacle to reform.

Mr. Harry J. Anslinger became head of the Bureau when it was first organized in 1930 and was not replaced until 1962, when Henry L. Giordano was named as his successor.

Under the reign of Commissioner Anslinger, any individual investigator who found himself at odds with the comprehensive official line laid down by the Bureau had to contend with the solid, monolithic phalanxes of the government bureaucracy. The latter, with the mass media and government printing presses available to them, could readily brand the heretic as an irresponsible "self-appointed expert," or inspire a stooge to attack him or to label his work "unscientific." As a result, discussion of the narcotics question during the Anslinger era was a dialogue between two schools of thought, those who agreed with the Bureau and those who did not.

The President's Advisory Commission recommended in 1963 that the government actively disseminate information concerning addiction and the drug problem in order to counteract mistaken popular ideas. At the White House Conference in 1962 a constantly recurring theme was that popular misconceptions greatly increased the difficulty of dealing with the problem and various remedial programs were suggested. The ironic aspect of this was that, to a very large extent, popular stereotypes in this area were based on ideas disseminated by the government, i.e., the Federal Bureau of Narcotics.

At the same time that the Bureau was promulgating a philosophy of addiction and harassing or maintaining surveillance over its critics, it conspicuously failed to provide reliable statistical information on its own enforcement activities or on the narcotics problem in general. It does not seem credible that the extremely poor statistical reporting of the Bureau could be due to lack of funds, for Congress was extremely generous to it in this respect and has apparently never questioned the Bureau's substantial public relations expenditures. It would appear that if the Bureau is not to be dismantled, it would be highly desirable that it put more money and manpower into improvement of its statistical services.

The so-called Advisory Committee to the Federal Bureau of Narcotics which Mr. Anslinger created to reply to an unfavorable American Bar Association-American Medical Association Joint Committee Report consisted mainly of police and prosecuting officials and others throughout the nation who agree with the Bureau's conception of the drug problem. The result of their work was a

symposium of intemperate and vituperative criticism of the Joint
Committee, its work, and of other persons known to be in some degree sympathetic with its viewpoint. This report was published in
1959 with a title, format, and color which made it hard to distinguish from the Interim Report itself. It was sold by the Super-
intendent of Documents for sixty cents and distributed gratis by
the Bureau of Narcotics and by some members of Congress. Official
circulation of the document was discontinued when the *Washington
Post* in 1960 gave publicity to a criticism of the Supreme Court
which it contained. Unofficially, according to Benjamin De Mott,
this publication, which he suggested "may well be the crudest publication yet produced by a government agency," continued to be
circulated. In a copy secured after official circulation had ceased,
the offending sentence had been crayoned out with black crayon
but was still legible. It was a statement made by Mr. Malachi
L. Harney, a former assistant of Mr. Anslinger's: "We are presently
the victims of a Supreme Court majority which to me seems almost
hysterical in its desire to suppress all freedom of action by law
enforcement officers."

According to De Mott, the Bureau's efforts to discourage the
publication of the Interim Report were terminated by an order
from the White House. It is possible that the publicity given the
incident by the press was also an important factor, for it was picked
up by countless newspapers and commentators. De Mott also stated
that the Bureau had consulted with officials of the Russell Sage
Foundation, apparently attempting to exert pressure upon them.

PHYSICIANS AND JUDGES AS SCAPEGOATS

Professor Benjamin De Mott, who has provided a description of
the top officials of the Federal Narcotics Bureau of the Anslinger
era, refers to the "fury of the Bureau's anti-intellectualism." Mr.
De Mott finds the roots of the Bureau's attitudes in what he calls
the "cop mentality." "Bureau officials," he says, "have a taste for
public propaganda that panders to provincial superstition of 'un-
American' types. . . . [T]he Bureau's dismissal of its critics is often
accompanied by an appeal to everything that is mean, ignorant,
and illiberal in the American consciousness. . . . Narcotics Bureau
propaganda reeks with station-house hints that any man who interests himself in the problem of 'known criminals' must have un-
savory reasons for doing so."

It has been pointed out that the Bureau has hammered away at the idea that judges were responsible for the postwar rise of addiction because of excessive leniency in imposing sentences, and, on the other hand, that the police are to be credited with the alleged decline of addiction during the decades before the war, when judges were just as lenient as later. These outrageous and inconsistent attempts to pass the buck have largely gone unchallenged and appear to have been accepted with little question by Congress. The underlying conception seems to have been that the competence of a judge is directly proportional to the severity of the sentences he imposes, regardless of individual circumstances, and that it is his duty in handling narcotics cases, at least, to follow the advice of the police.

THE POLICY POSITION OF THE PUBLIC HEALTH SERVICE

With infrequent exceptions, narcotics officials of the Public Health Service, in their public utterances on policy matters, have supported the position of the Federal Bureau of Narcotics and joined forces with it in assailing critics of the status quo. Students seeking information and bibliographical references on the drug problem from the Public Health Service have ordinarily been provided with articles written by its officials and with bibliographies consisting largely of Public Health Service publications plus a few by Bureau spokesmen and outsiders who support the Bureau's position. Bureau publications are ordinarily deferred to as authoritative with respect to questions of enforcement, while those of the Public Health Service officials are regarded as authoritative on the medical, psychiatric, and biological aspects of addiction. The Bureau reciprocates by referring students to Public Health Service publications and provides them with packets of reprints by its officials. Neither agency provides references to materials not in conformity with the official line established by the Bureau.

MONKEYS ON THE ADDICT'S BACK

It is axiomatic among students of human behavior that once certain institutional arrangements have been made and are established they tend to be extremely resistant to change. One of the reasons for this is that vested interests develop; persons, groups, associations, and organizations find that they are benefiting in one way or another from existing arrangements. They consequently oppose change, but in doing so rarely mention the real grounds for their conservatism—indeed, they are sometimes unaware of the influence of self-interest. Significant change or improvement in institutional arrangements therefore invariably arouses opposition for the very good reason that such change means that there will be a price to pay, that some persons will lose jobs, power, prestige, or money and that others may gain these things.

The President's Advisory Commission recommended in its report that "the definition of legitimate medical use of narcotic drugs and legitimate medical treatment of a narcotic addict are primarily to be determined by the medical profession." The Commission completely ignored the 1963 report of the New York Academy of Medicine dealing directly with this matter. Instead, it asked the American Medical Association and the National Research Council of the National Academy of Sciences to make a statement on the issue. The result was a masterpiece of diplomacy and noncommittal doubletalk, and was published as part of the report of the Presidential Commission. It stipulated that it is the duty of doctors to obey all laws, rules and regulations at federal, state, and local levels, and simply reiterated the current regulations of the Treasury Department as the definition of proper medical treatment of addicts, without indicating that the definition was drawn from Treasury Department regulations.

The Commission evidently assumed that the A.M.A.–N.R.C. report automatically made the view of the New York Academy unacceptable and illegitimate. But proper medical treatment of diseased persons is not something which is settled by majority vote of A.M.A. officials. That body cannot and does not dictate to physicians how they are to treat diseases. Such questions, like scientific questions, are never settled by majority vote. If they were, and departures from sanctioned practice were prosecuted in the criminal courts as they are in this instance, there could be little progress. The President's Commission, despite its gesture to the medical profession, clearly did not accept the idea of full medical control as advocated by the New York Academy of Medicine. That was no doubt why it made no reference whatever to that organization's position.

The President's Commission, instead of proposing any plan which would have given physicians the authority they must have if addiction is not to be handled punitively, recommended a program of civil commitment, not as a substitute for imprisonment, but as an alternative to it in selected instances. The Attorney General and the Judiciary, it suggests, should make the "crucial determinations" at the federal level and the Bureau of Prisons, the Public Health Service, and the probation and parole services should manage the actual program. This program explicitly avoids giving any important authority to medical persons. It also leaves the addict's status under the criminal law unchanged, does nothing to remove the threat of prosecution for doctors, and leaves the hapless user in the hands of the illicit traffic.

c h a p t e r   f o u r

Criminalizing marijuana:
the crusade continues

DONALD T. DICKSON

The occurrence of a moral commitment within a bureaucratic setting is not an uncommon phenomenon, especially in our federal bureaucratic system. Examples abound, including the Federal Bureau of Investigation, the Bureau of Narcotics, the Selective Service System, the Central Intelligence Agency, the Internal Revenue Service, and—on a different scale—the Departments of State and Justice. In fact, one could argue that some sort of moral commitment is necessary for the effective functioning of any bureaucratic body. Usually this moral commitment is termed an "ideology" and is translated into goals for the bureaucracy. Anthony Downs suggests four uses for an ideology: 1) to influence outsiders to support the bureau or at least not attack it; 2) to develop a goal consensus among the bureau members; 3) to facilitate a selective recruitment of staff, that is, to attract those who will support and further the goals of the bureau and repel those who would detract from those goals; and 4) to provide an alternative in decision making where other choice criteria are impratical or ambiguous.[1]

While most if not all bureaucracies attempt to maintain this moral commitment or ideology for the above mentioned reasons, some go further and initiate moral crusades, whereby they attempt to instill this commitment into groups and individuals outside their

Abridged from pp. 143–56 "Bureaucracy and Morality: An Organizational Perspective on a Moral Crusade," by Donald T. Dickson. From *Social Problems* XVI, 143 (1968). Reprinted by permission of the author and the publisher.

[1] Anthony Downs, *Inside Bureaucracy*, Boston: Little, Brown, 1967.

bureaus. The Narcotics Bureau in its efforts to mold public and congressional opinion against drug use is one bureaucratic example, the F.B.I. in its anti-subversive and anti-communist crusades another.[2] The question then becomes, under what conditions does this transference of ideology from the bureaucracy to its environment or specific groups within its environment take place? Howard S. Becker supplies one answer to this, suggesting that this is the work of a "moral entrepreneur," either in the role of a crusading reformer or a rule enforcer.[3] In either role, the moral entrepreneur as an individual takes the initiative and generates a "moral enterprise."

The difference between the moral entrepreneur situation and a situation wherein the moral crusade results primarily from a bureaucratic response to environmental factors, is that in the latter instance moral considerations are secondary to bureaucratic survival and growth, while in the former instance moral considerations are primary. Further, the end results of either of these crusades may vary considerably since each is in response to different stimuli. Other conditions being equal, the bureaucratic crusade will continue only as long as bureaucratic considerations dictate, while the moral crusade will continue as long as the individual moral crusader's zealotry requires.

In this paper, the work of the Bureau of Narcotics and its former commissioner, Harry J. Anslinger, are examined in light of Becker's conclusion that Anslinger was a moral entrepreneur who led his Bureau on a moral crusade against the use of marihuana, culminating in an Anslinger-instigated publicity campaign that persuaded first the general public and then Congress that marihuana use was a vicious habit that should be outlawed and severely penalized.[4] Given the short time span Becker chose and his individualized focus, this seems to be a logical explanation of the Bureau's efforts. Given a broader organizational perspective, however, the passage of the Marihuana Tax Act and the Bureau's part in that passage appear to be only one phase of a larger organizational process, that of environmental change.

[2] Fred J. Cook, *The FBI Nobody Knows*, New York: Macmillan, 1964.
[3] Howard S. Becker, *The Outsiders: Studies in the Sociology of Deviance*, New York: Free Press, 1963, esp. pp. 147–163.
[4] Becker, *op. cit.*, pp. 135–146.

ORGANIZATIONS AND ENVIRONMENTS

One on-going problem an organization must cope with is its relationship with its environment. If the organization wishes to grow and expand or even continue to exist, it must come to terms with its environment, and where necessary insure acceptance by it. No doubt a few organizations with substantial resources may exist for some time in a hostile environment, but the more normal case seems to be that an organization must at least establish an environmentally neutral relationship if not an environmentally supportive one.

Of course when the organization is in its incipient stages, the problems are magnified. Environmental support is more necessary, environmental hostility more of a threat to survival. Usually the organization will adapt to the demands of the environment, but occasionally the organization either chooses to attempt to alter these demands, or chooses to ignore them. Not uncommonly such a decision results in drastic consequences for the organization.

An organization may attempt to alter the demands of its environment when such an attempt would not draw too heavily upon the organization's resources, or when the alternative, adaptation to the environment, would mean a substantial loss to the organization or perhaps dissolution.

Organizational attempts at environmental change will depend upon a number of factors:

(a) The necessity for change—is environmental change a prerequisite for organizational survival, or is it not necessary but merely desirable?

(b) The amount of resources available—can the organization afford to attempt the change effort?

(c) The size and complexity of the environment—would change be necessary in only a small element in the environment, or would a whole complex of elements need to be altered?

(d) The extent to which change must take place—is it necessary to change only some environmental policy or practice, or is it necessary to totally revamp the environmental structure from values on down?

(e) Is the policy, goal, norm, or value to be changed, strongly or weakly held—is it firmly entrenched and legitimated, or is it "precarious?"

In his discussion of the Marihuana Tax Act as a "moral enterprise," Becker was concerned with a weakly-held value, as will be shown, though he did not discuss it in these terms.

A CASE STUDY: THE U.S. BUREAU
OF NARCOTICS

THE BUREAU AS A PUBLIC BUREAUCRACY

This case study will be limited to an analysis of the policies of the Narcotics Bureau and the effects of these policies on salient elements of its environment. In its efforts to mold public opinion in support of its policies, it is not unlike many organizations, especially those with a moral commitment. The W.C.T.U. carried on the same sort of campaign—including propaganda, attacks on its critics, and legislative lobbying. What makes the Bureau unique from many other organizations which have tried to influence their environments is that the campaign was and is carried out by a governmental organ.

Several ramifications of this difference are immediately apparent. There is the element of legitimation. The public is far more likely to accept the pronouncements of a federal department than a voluntary private organization. There is the element of propaganda development. Due to its public nature, a federal department is more skilled in dealing with the public and in preparing propaganda for public consumption. There is the element of communication. A federal organization has far more means available for the dissemination of the information than a private one—by press releases, publications, or lectures and speeches—and it is likely to have representatives based in major population centers to disseminate the information. There is the element of coercion. A federal department can bring a wide range of pressures to bear on its critics.

Finally, at a different level, a federal bureau differs in the area of survival. Private organizations have considerable control over their future. They may decide to expand, continue as before, disband, merge, alter their aims, or reduce their activities. A federal department may go through any of the above stages, but frequently the final decision does not rest within the department but with the congressional, executive, or judicial body that created it. A bureau created by congressional enactment will continue to be unaltered except by internal decision only as long as Congress can be convinced that there is no need to alter it. Although there may be some question of degree, there is no question that public opinion will be a major factor in the congressional decision.

Therefore the federal department must convince the public and Congress: 1) that it serves a useful, or if possible, a necessary function; and 2) that it is uniquely qualified to do so. The less the department is sure of its future status, the more it will try to convince Congress and the public of these.

BACKGROUND TO ENVIRONMENTAL CHANGE: THE EMERGENCE AND DEVELOPMENT OF THE BUREAU

In the late nineteenth and early twentieth centuries, narcotics were widely available: through doctors who indiscriminately prescribed morphine and later heroin as pain killers, through druggists who sold them openly, or through a wide variety of patent medicines.

A narcotics division was created in the Internal Revenue Bureau of the Treasury Department to collect revenue and enforce the Harrison Act. In 1920 it merged into the Prohibition Unit of that department and upon its creation in 1927 into the Prohibition Bureau. In 1930 the Bureau of Narcotics was formed as a separate Bureau in the Treasury Department.

LEGITIMATION: THE PROCESS OF CHANGING AN ENVIRONMENT

After 1914 the powers of the Narcotics Division were clear and limited: to enforce registration and record-keeping, violation of which could result in imprisonment for up to ten years, and to supervise revenue collection. The large number of addicts who secured their drugs from physicians were excluded from the Division's jurisdiction. The public's attitude toward drug use had not changed much with the passage of the Act—there was some opposition to drug use, some support of it, and a great many who did not care one way or the other. In fact, the Harrison Act was passed with very little publicity or news coverage.[5]

Thus at this time the Narcotics Division was faced with a severely restricted scope of operations. Acceptance of the legislation as envisioned by Congress would mean that the Division would at best continue as a marginal operation with limited enforcement duties. Given the normal, well-documented bureaucratic tendency toward growth and expansion, and given the fact that the Division was a public bureaucracy and needed to justify its operations and usefulness before Congress, it would seem that increased power and jurisdiction in the area of drug control would be a desirable and, in fact, necessary goal. Adaptation to the Harrison Act limitations would preclude attainment of this goal. Operating under a legislative mandate, the logical alternative to adaptation would be to persuade the Congress and public that expansion was necessary and to extend the provisions of the Harrison Act.

Also at this point, the public's attitude toward narcotics use could be characterized as only slightly opposed. Faced with a situation where adaptation to the existing legislation was bureaucratically unfeasible, where expansion was desirable, and where environmental support—from both Congress and the public—was necessary for continued existence, the Division launched a twopronged campaign: 1) a barrage of reports and newspaper articles which generated a substantial public outcry against narcotics use, and 2) a series of Division-sponsored test cases in the courts which resulted in a reinterpretation of the Harrison Act and substantially broadened powers for the Narcotics Division.[6] Thus the Division attained its goals by altering a weakly-held public value regarding narcotics use from neutrality or slight opposition to strong opposition, and by persuading the courts that it should have increased powers.[7]

[5] The *New York Times Index* for 1914 lists only two brief articles on the federal legislation, one in June and one in August when the Senate adopted the Act. It should be noted that there was also discussion of a broadened New York State narcotics act and articles publicizing the arrest of violators of an earlier New York statute at that time.

[6] King, *op. cit.*, pp. 737–748, Lindesmith, *The Addict . . .* , pp. 5–11.

[7] In focusing on judicial expansion of existing legislation rather than on further Congressional action, the Division was able to avoid the lobbies of doctors and pharmacists who strongly opposed the Harrison Act in the first place and

Though the resources of the Division were limited, it was able to accomplish its goals because it was a public bureaucracy and as such had the aforementioned advantages which arise from that status. Since the ability to develop propaganda and the means to communicate it were inherent in this status, as was the propensity by the public to accept this propaganda, environmental support could be generated with less resource expenditure. Further, the Division as a public bureaucracy would be assumed to have a familiarity with governmental processes not only in its own executive branch, but also in the congressional and judicial branches as well. This built-in expertise necessary for the Division's expansion might be quite costly in time and resources for the private bureaucracy but again was inherent in the Division's status.

One typical example of the public campaign was a report cited and relied upon by the Narcotics Division for some years. It is an interesting combination of truth, speculation, and fiction, a mix which the Division and the Bureau which succeeded it found to be an effective public persuader for many years. In a report dated June, 1919, a committee appointed by the Treasury Department to study narcotics reported *inter alia* that there were 237,665 addicts in the United States treated by physicians (based upon a 30 percent response by physicians queried), that there were over one million addicts in the country in 1919 (a figure based upon a compromise between projections based on the percentage of addicts in Jacksonville, Florida in 1913 and New York City in 1918), that there was extensive addiction among children, that narcotics were harmful to health and morals, and that they were directly connected with crime and abject poverty. Among the physical effects noted were insanity; diseased lungs, hearts, and kidneys; rotting of the skin; and sterility.[8]

This "scholarly report" is an interesting example of the propaganda effort, for it appears to the casual reader to be credible (especially given its source), and contains charges which seem to be designed to generate widespread public disgust toward narcotics users and support for the Division and its efforts. Many of the same

---

who successfully lobbied for the medical exception. See the *New York Times*, June 28, 1914, Sec. II, p. 5.

[8] U.S. Treasury Department, *Report of Special Committee to Investigate the Traffic in Narcotic Drugs* (April 15, 1919).

ction was carrying out its public campaign, it was
also busy in the courts. Between 1918 and 1921 the Narcotics
Division won three important cases in the Supreme Court and persuaded the Court, essentially, to delete the medical exception from
the Harrison Act thereby broadening its position as an enforcement
agency. In the first case, *Webb v. United States*,[9] the court held
that a physician could not supply narcotics to an addict unless he
was attempting to cure him and in so doing made illegal the work
of a large number of physicians who were supplying addicts with
drugs under the registration procedures of the Harrison Act. This
decision was supported in the two following cases: *Jin Fuey Moy
v. United States*[10] and *United States v. Behrman*.[11] In *Behrman*,
it was held that physicians could not even supply drugs to addicts
in an attempt to cure them. The medical exception was nullified.
The cases were skillfully chosen and presented to the court. Each
was a flagrant abuse of the statute—in *Webb*, the physician's professional practice seemed to be limited to supplying narcotics to
whoever wanted them. In the other two cases, the physicians supplied huge amounts of drugs over short periods of time to a small
number of patients—patently for resale at a later time. Yet the
Division did not argue for and the court did not rule on the cases
as violations of the statute as it was intended, but instead regarded
all of these as normal professional practices by physicians and held
that, as such, they were illegal.

Three years after *Behrman*, the court somewhat reversed itself in
Linder v. United States.[12] Here the doctor supplied a small dosage
to a patient who was a government informer. The court rejected
the government's case in a unanimous opinion, holding:

The enactment under consideration . . . says nothing of "addicts" and
does not undertake to prescribe methods for their medical treatment, and
we cannot possibly conclude that a physician acted improperly or unwisely
or for other than medical purposes solely because he has dispensed to one

9 249 *U.S.* 96 (1918).
10 254 *U.S.* 189 (1920).
11 259 *U.S.* 280 (1921).
12 268 *U.S.* 5 (1924).

of them, in the ordinary course and in good faith, four small tablets of morphine or cocaine for relief of condition incident to addiction.[13]

The court went on to warn the Division:

Federal power is delegated, and its prescribed limits must not be transcended even though the ends seem desirable. The unfortunate condition of the recipient certainly created no reasonable probability that she would sell or otherwise dispose of the few tablets entrusted to her and we cannot say that by so dispensing them the doctor necessarily transcended the limits of that professional conduct with which Congress never intended to interfere.[14]

Though *Linder* might have reintroduced doctors into the area, the Narcotics Division successfully prevented this by refusing to recognize *Linder* in its regulations, thus creating a situation where few would accept the risks involved in testing the doctrine, and by launching an all-out campaign against doctors—closing the remaining narcotics clinics, imprisoning rebellious doctors, and publicizing records and convictions of physician addicts.[15]

Rufus King comments on this period of growth:

In sum, the Narcotics Division succeeded in creating a very large criminal class for itself to police . . . instead of the very small one Congress has intended.[16]

The success of this campaign was reflected not only in the increased number of potential criminals, but in financial growth as well. Between 1918 and 1925, the Bureau's budgetary appropriations increased from $325,000 to $1,329,440, a rise of over 400 percent.[17]

[13] 268 *U.S.* 5 at 15 (1924).
[14] 268 *U.S.* 5 at 20 (1924).
[15] King, *op. cit.*, pp. 744–745; "Note: Narcotics Regulation . . . ," pp. 784–787. The Bureau's yearly report *Traffic in Opium and Other Dangerous Drugs* carries numerous reports of addiction among physicians during this period. See also Lindesmith, *The Addict* . . . , pp. 135–161.
[16] King, *op. cit.*, p. 738.
[17] See Table 1. During this period, two pieces of legislation were enacted that affected the Bureau's scope of operation: The Revenue Act of 1918, and the Narcotic Drug Import and Export Act of 1922.

THE MARIHUANA TAX ACT OF 1937:
A BUREAUCRATIC RESPONSE

There are many other examples of efforts by the Bureau to create and maintain a friendly and supportive environment—through other publicity campaigns, through lobbying in Congress, and through continued and diligent attacks upon and harassments of its critics—which have been amply chronicled by others, although not as part of an organizational process.[18]

The Bureau's efforts to induce passage of the Marihuana Tax Act deserve special mention, however, in light of Becker's finding that the legislation was the result of what he terms a "moral enterprise." [19] Becker concludes that Narcotics Commissioner Anslinger and his Bureau were the motive forces behind the original 1937 legislation and the increasingly severe penalties which have since been imposed. This is readily conceded.[20] But he argues that the motivation behind this desire for the marihuana legislation was a moral one. He presents a picture of a society totally indifferent to the use of marihuana until Anslinger, in the role of a moral entrepreneur, "blows the whistle" on marihuana smoking. Again, it is conceded that Commissioner Anslinger throughout his long career with the Narcotics Bureau has opposed drug and narcotics use on moral grounds. This theme runs consistently through his writings.[21] What Becker ignores is that Anslinger was also a bureau-

---

[18] Along with the works of Lindesmith and King above, see the Bureau's publication, *Comments on Narcotic Drugs* (undated), the Bureau's reply to the A.B.A.-A.M.A. committee interim report "Narcotic Drugs." This publication was described by DeMott as "perhaps the crudest publication yet produced by a government agency . . ." and was later taken out of print. Benjamin DeMott, "The Great Narcotics Muddle," *Harpers Magazine*, March, 1962, p. 53. For a vivid account of the Bureau's methods with its critics, see Lindesmith, *The Addict* . . . , pp. 242–268.

[19] Becker, *op. cit.*, p. 135.

[20] It seems clear from examining periodicals, newspapers, and the *Congressional Record* that the Bureau was primarily responsible for the passage of the act, though Becker's almost exclusive reliance on the claims of the Bureau in its official publication *Traffic in Opium and Other Dangerous Drugs* does not seem warranted given the previously discussed tendency of a public bureaucracy to emphasize its necessity and successful functioning.

[21] See especially Harry Anslinger and Will Osborne, *The Murderers: The Story of the Narcotic Gang*, New York: Farrar, Straus, 1961, Chap. 1; and also the other writings of the Commissioner, among them: Harry Anslinger and William F. Tompkins, *The Traffic in Narcotics*, New York: Funk and Wagnalls,

80   *Donald T. Dickson*

crat and thus responsive to bureaucratic pressures and demands as well. The distinction between these roles is difficult to make but it is fundamental in analyzing the legislation.

The Marihuana Tax Act which imposed a prohibitively costly tax on the sale of marihuana was passed by both houses of Congress with practically no debate[22] and signed into law on August 2, 1937. While Becker seems to argue that the Bureau generated a great public outcry against marihuana use prior to the passage of the Act, his data supporting this argument are misleading if not erroneously interpreted.[23] While marihuana use seems to have increased since the early 1930's, there appears to have been little public concern expressed in the news media, even in 1937. Few magazine articles were written about the subject, and if the *New York Times* is any indication, newspaper coverage was also slight.[24] The

---

1953; and Harry Anslinger and J. Gregory, *The Protectors: The Heroic Story of the Narcotic Agents, Citizens and Officials in Their Unending, Unsung Battle Against Organized Crime in America*, New York: Farrar, Straus, 1964.

[22] This is not unusual in the area of moral legislation, as Becker points out. Furthermore, unlike non-criminal legislation where the losing party still has a variety of remedies available to challenge the law, few remedies are available to those who are legislated against in criminal areas. Legitimate lobbies cannot be formed and test cases are dangerous.

However, Becker gives the impression that the only opposition to the marihuana legislation came from hemp growers, and that no one argued for the marihuana users (*Outsiders*, pp. 144–145). This is erroneous. The legislative counsel for the A.M.A., Dr. William C. Woodward, challenged the Bureau's conclusions that marihuana use was harmful to health and widespread among children, and demanded evidence to support these assertions. While he was not representing the marihuana users, he was certainly arguing their case and questioning the need for the legislation. See *Taxation of Marihuana*, Hearings Before the Committee on Ways and Means of the House of Representatives, 75th Congress, 1st Session, on H.R. 6385, April 27–30 and May 4, 1937, esp. p. 92. It should be noted that this opposition was ignored by the committee members.

[23] Becker's data consist of a survey of the *Readers Guide to Periodical Literature*, in which he found that no magazine articles appeared before July, 1935; four appeared between July, 1935 and June, 1937; and 17 between July, 1937 and June, 1939 (*Outsiders*, p. 141). While this is correct, it is misleading due to the time intervals used. The four articles in the second period all appeared before 1937, no articles appeared in the five months preceding the House committee hearings on the act in late April and early May, one appeared in July, 1937, and the rest appeared after the bill was signed into law on August 2, 1937. In short, of the articles which Becker asserts provided the impetus to Congressional action, only one appeared in the seven months of 1937 before the marihuana bill was signed into law.

[24] A survey of the *New York Times Index* shows: one article discussed marihuana in 1936 and eight discussed the subject between January and August

final presidential signing of the act received minimal coverage from the *Times*.[25] In short, rather than the Bureau-generated public turmoil that Becker indicates, it seems that public awareness of the problem, as well as public opposition to it, was slight.

While it cannot be shown conclusively that the Marihuana Tax Act was the result of a bureaucratic response to environmental conditions, similarities between this period and the post-Harrison Act period are evident. Marihuana opposition, like narcotics opposition before, appears to have resulted from a weakly held value. In both situations, publicity campaigns were launched. In both cases, one through the courts and one through Congress, efforts were exerted to expand the power of the Bureau. In both cases, there were substantial numbers of potential criminals who could be incorporated into the Bureau's jurisdiction.

Perhaps more convincing than similarities are the budgetary appropriations for the Bureau from 1915 to 1944 presented in Table 1. In 1932, when the Bureau's appropriations were approaching an all time high, the Bureau stated:

The present constitutional limitations would seem to require control measures directed against the intrastate traffic of Indian hemp (marihuana) to be adopted by the several State governments rather than by the Federal Government, and the policy has been to urge the State authorities generally to provide the necessary legislation, with supporting enforcement activity, to prohibit the traffic except for bona fide medical purposes. The proposed uniform State narcotic law . . . with optional text applying to restriction of traffic in Indian hemp, has been recommended as an adequate law to accomplish the desired purpose.

At this time, according to the Bureau, sixteen states had enacted legislation in which "the sale or possession (of marihuana) is prohibited except for medical purposes." One year later, 18 more states had enacted the desired legislation, and by 1936, it appears that the

---

1937. There were no articles about or coverage of any of the Congressional hearings. Contrary to Becker's assertion, perhaps the most significant thing about this period was the lack of publicity involved.

[25] The total coverage by the *New York Times* consisted of a four line AP dispatch near the bottom of page four, titled "Signs Bill to Curb Marihuana" and reading in its entirety: "President Roosevelt signed today a bill to curb traffic in the narcotic, marihuana, through heavy taxes on transactions." (August 3, 1937.)

TABLE 1. BUDGETARY APPROPRIATIONS FOR THE U.S. NARCOTICS
BUREAU (1915–1944)*

Year**	Total Appropriation
1915	$ 292,000
1916	300,000
1917	325,000
1918	750,000
1919	750,000
1920	750,000
1921	750,000
1922	750,000
1923	750,000
1924	1,250,000
1925	1,329,440
1926	1,329,440
1927	1,329,440
1928	1,329,440
1929	1,350,440
1930	1,411,260
1931	1,611,260
1932	1,708,528
1933	1,525,000
1934	1,400,000
1935	1,244,899
1936	1,249,470
1937	1,275,000
1938	1,267,000
1939	1,267,600
1940	1,306,700
1941	1,303,280
1942	1,283,975
1943	1,289,060
1944	1,150,000

* Source: Appropriations Committee, U.S. Senate, *Appropriations, New Offices,*
etc., Statements Showing Appropriations Made, New Offices Created, etc., 1915–
1923; U.S. Bureau of the Budget, *The Budget of the United States Government,*
Washington: Government Printing Office, 1923–1945.
** Fiscal year the appropriation was made. Each sum was appropriated for the
following fiscal year.

Bureau's policy had succeeded completely for all 48 states had
enacted legislation which governed the sale or possession of marihuana.

Despite this apparent success and despite former questions concerning the constitutionality of the measure, the Bureau in 1937
pressed for the enactment of the federal marihuana act. For Anslinger, the moral entrepreneur, 1936 should have been a year of

victory. In every state the marihuana menace was subjected to statutory control. But for Anslinger, the bureaucrat, 1936 seems to have been another year of defeat. His budgetary appropriation remained near a low point that had not been seen in over a decade, which to some extent reflected the general economic conditions of the time. His request for fiscal 1933 had been cut $100,000 below the general Treasury Department reduction for all bureaus.[26] In succeeding years, reductions in actual operating expenses were greater than those reflected in Table 1, for varying sums were deducted from the appropriations and held in a general trust fund as part of the government's anti-depression program. The Bureau's actual operating funds remained at about one million dollars from fiscal 1934 to fiscal 1936. In his appearances before the House Subcommittee of the Committee on Appropriations that considered the Treasury Department budget, Anslinger repeatedly warned that the limited budget was curtailing his enforcement activities.[27] By 1936, his budget had decreased over $450,000 from its high four years before, a fall of almost 26 percent.

Again in 1937 Anslinger, the moralist, would be expected first to convince the general public that marihuana use was evil and immoral, while Anslinger, the bureaucrat, would be more concerned with attaining passage of legislation which would increase the Bureau's powers and then proceed to generate environmental support for these powers. In fact, the latter occurred. The great bulk of Bureau-inspired publicity came after the passage of the act, not before.

[26] *Hearings Before the Subcommittee of the House Committee on Appropriations*, 72nd Congress, 1st Session, in charge of the Treasury Department Appropriations Bill for 1933, January 14, 1932, pp. 375–393.

[27] Thus in the hearing for the 1935 appropriation:

Mr. Arnold: How are you getting by with that $1,000,000 after those deductions?

Comm. Anslinger: I am getting by, but I have had to cut back enforcement activities so sharply that it has reached a point where I think it has been harmful . . . (1935 Hearings, *op. cit.*, p. 189).

In his opening statement at the hearing for the 1936 appropriation, Anslinger stated "Mr. Chairman, and distinguished members of the committee, during the past fiscal year we have been operating under a very restricted appropriation. Our enforcement did not fall off too much although it did suffer somewhat." (1936 Hearings, *op. cit.*, p. 201.) A decrease in seizures and fines levied was attributed to the limited budget, *ibid.*, pp. 213–214.

Faced with a steadily decreasing budget, the Bureau responded as any organization so threatened might react: it tried to appear more necessary, and it tried to increase its scope of operations. As a result of this response, the Marihuana Tax Act of 1937 was passed.[28] Whether the Bureau's efforts were entirely successful is questionable. One beneficial result for the Bureau was that violations and seizures under the Marihuana Tax Act contributed substantially to the Bureau's totals, which had been declining for some time. (When arrests, convictions, and seizures were on the increase, these were faithfully reported to the House Subcommittee as evidence of the Bureau's effective use of funds.) In 1938, the first full year under the Marihuana Tax Act, one out of every four federal drug and narcotic convictions was for a marihuana violation.

Financially, the enterprise was less successful. Though the budgetary decline was halted, expected increases for enforcing the new legislation did not immediately materialize. Anslinger pointed out this problem in a 1937 subcommittee hearing in connection with the fiscal 1939 appropriation:

COMM. ANSLINGER: We took on the administration of the marihuana law and did not get any increase for that purpose. The way we are running we may have to request a deficiency of $100,000 at the end of the year; but I sincerely hope you will not see me here for a deficit. Beginning the first of the year, Mr. Chairman, I shall control all travel out of Washington. That is a hard job. I have to do that to make up some of this money. We went ahead at high speed and broke up ten big distributing rings, and now we find ourselves in the hole financially.

MR. LUDLOW: You have to find some way to recoup?

COMM. ANSLINGER: Yes; and keep the enforcement of the Marihuana Act going. Not a dollar has been appropriated in connection with the enforcement of the Marihuana law. We have taken on the work in connection with the Marihuana Act in addition to our other duties.

In conclusion, it should be reiterated that this paper does not presume to refute the moral entrepreneur approach—for in many instances it is a valid and useful means of analysis—but rather it

---

[28] While Commissioner Anslinger as leader of this bureaucratic response might be characterized as a "bureaucratic entrepreneur," such characterization would be misleading, for similar to Becker's characterization it still simplifies the problem by emphasizing the individual's importance rather than that of the Bureau and its environment.

attempts to demonstrate an alternative explanation that may frequently be appropriate. It would be either naive or presumptuous to deny that some combination of both moral and bureaucratic factors exist in any given crusade.

III
Private components of the establishment

The role of nongovernment power holders—especially economic ones—in the crime-control establishment has never been seriously documented. The sociologist William J. Chambliss has argued that:

> Conventional myths notwithstanding, the history of the criminal law is *not* a history of public opinion or public interest being reflected in criminal-law legislation. On the contrary, the history of the criminal law is everywhere the history of legislation and appellate-court decisions which in effect (if not in intent) reflect the interests of the economic elites who control the production and distribution of the major resources of the society.

Admittedly, Chambliss has succumbed to the temptation to overgeneralize (an understandable one, given the uniqueness of his insight) and it is difficult to sustain his thesis for the entire broad spectrum of the criminal law. Law is an amalgam of diverse concerns and varying interests (some of them moral and apparently unrelated to economic elitist desires). The law often reflects the ability of particular groups to form coalitions that enable them to legislate their own concerns into rules that bind an entire society (indeed, Prohibition was the last gasp of an earlier, rural, fundamentalist America in response to their loss of economic power and social prestige).

Also, much law exists simply because of the factor of social inertia (a particularly important factor here because of our cultural belief that "the law" should embody "everlasting" concerns) and an unwillingness to recognize that society often changes rapidly. Certainly the desires and needs of economic elites play a major (often *the* major) role in lawmaking, but there are simply too many areas of the criminal law which are of no interest to such elites or which cause elites to split.

Perhaps it is more meaningful to speak of "key" groups— most of which doubtlessly reflect dominant economic interests, influence crime control, cooperate on local levels with criminal justice agencies, and provide public support to both the national crime-control establishment and their local satellites (since all of these groups are conservative). While evidence about the real function of these "key" groups in the crime-control process is scanty, there can be no doubt that (a) such a function exists and that (b) it is a vital part of our perpetual war against crime. As the McKay Commission noted:

> Under a state law adopted at the urging of organized labor, goods made in prison can only be sold to the state, state agencies, and municipalities. . . .
> Conditions in the metal shops at Attica precluded for all but a few any hope of achieving vocational skills and good work habits. Featherbedding was the main problem; supervisors had no control over the number of men assigned to the shops and there was work for only 250 of the 450 inmates assigned [to the metal shop] at the time of the uprising.

We do not yet know much about the importance of business's views of crime, but the role of private business groups, especially when they band together in local and state crime commissions, is not insignificant. Some aspects of this activity are described by Robert Cipes, a former Justice Department prosecutor, in the excerpt from his book *The Crime War.*

chapter five

Crime control and economic elites

ROBERT M. CIPES

The backlash sentiment, which Goldwater tried to tap, is as potent in the upper-middle class as in the lower-middle. In both cases the motivation is largely economic. What conservatives are concerned with, as Richard Goodwin has pointed out, is not so much the exercise of authority but its content. A man can oppose the welfare state and at the same time support the police; one is threatening his property rights, the other protecting them. The policeman is his agent. Identity of interest between the citizen and the police may be formalized in the creation of a civic group to support local police. This is the entity known as the citizens' crime commission. It is a permanent action group, as opposed to groups like the President's Crime Commission, which is a temporary study group.

The first citizens' crime commission was established in Chicago in 1919. It was the offspring of the Association of Commerce, whose members were "men of big business affairs." Fighting crime, the Commission said, was good business, for "continuous, preventable crime is just as destructive of property values as a continual series of preventable fires, and the problem of reducing crime is just as much a business proposition as the problem of reducing loss by fire." The Commission newsletter eulogized its founders in these terms: "The word 'failure' was not in their dictionaries. When they undertook a war on crime it meant W-A-R. It also meant that the war would be won."

The tough-minded members of the Chicago Commission com-

Abridged from pp. 15–17 of *The Crime War*, by Robert M. Cipes. © 1968 by Robert M. Cipes. Reprinted by permission of The New American Library, Inc., New York, New York.

plained of "too much meddling by well-meaning people who do not understand crime and criminals." The Commission's own theories of criminology were simple. Since it considered heredity one of the chief causes of crime, the way to control crime was by sterilization and by eugenics laws, under which all applicants for marriage licenses would have to prove they were morally clean. Another cause of crime was the familiar one—"lack of respect for constituted authority." The Commission worked with the Board of Education and the Committee on Americanism to instill such respect in the city's schoolchildren. Its own brand of Americanism was typified by the slogan: "The United States continues to be a dumping ground for the riff-raff of Europe." Thus the Commission added immigration to its list of causes of crime.

Though the members of the Chicago Crime Commission often sounded like vigilantes, theirs was not the traditional form of frontier justice. They did not believe in taking the law into their own hands, in resorting to violence themselves, but they supported the exercise of violence by the authorities. Commission members were not a lynch mob as such; they simply applauded official hangings and lobbied bitterly against reprieves. Then, as now, indignant businessmen lobbied for tougher penalties. The theft of a car outraged them, and they tried to make every car theft punishable by a mandatory ten-year sentence. This proposal was rejected, but another Commission suggestion was adopted, fixing a minimum of one year and a maximum of twenty. Some convictions were obtained under this statute, but soon the public came to realize that most cars were taken by young boys on "joy rides." There was revulsion against the mandatory sentence. Prosecutors avoided using the statute, and when they did use it, judges and juries often refused to convict.

This backlash did not make the Crime Commission members happy. "Age must be forgotten and the matter treated as a menacing situation"; more thought should be given "to the feelings of the citizens who suffered at the hands of the car thief," ignoring that almost ninety percent of the cars were recovered shortly after they were taken. Without realizing it, the Crime Commission had become a front for the insurance companies, which wanted to keep their losses down. And inevitably the campaign of terror which the Commission mounted got out of control. Trigger-happy policemen killed several boys and seriously wounded others as they attempted to steal some cars. So the vigilantes had their way; the ultimate punishment had been inflicted for car theft.

Today in the District of Columbia the strongest lobbies for harsh criminal statutes are the Board of Trade and an association of bankers. These groups take full-page ads in newspapers, write letters to the President, testify before Congress, and make speeches throughout the city—all to propagandize the need for more police powers, more rigid criminal laws, and more severe sentences.

These activities are reminiscent of the first citizens crime commission, which was formed in Chicago almost fifty years ago. One of the first projects of the Chicago Crime Commission was to keep a running box score of convicts sentenced to hang; each month the Commission's bulletin reminded the authorities of how many men were left unexecuted. Chicago was plagued by organized crime and gang warfare in the twenties, so that businessmen were not imagining the existence of crime. The trouble was that, like most alarmists, they exaggerated the threat, lumping the social misfits and defectives with professional gangsters. Taking a list of "murderers" which the Commission published, Clarence Darrow showed that only a few of the homicides involved premeditated killings or gang murders. In the same article, Darrow wrote:

Readers of newspapers and periodicals are constantly regaled with lurid stories of crime. From time to time with great regularity these tales are pieced together to produce the impression that waves of crime are sweeping across the land. Long rows of figures generally go with these tales which purport to tabulate the number of murders, hold-ups, burglaries, etc., in given areas, and sometimes comparisons are drawn with other countries and with other periods. The general effect is always to arouse anger and hatred, to induce legislatures to pass more severe laws, to fill the jails and penitentiaries, and to furnish more victims for the electric chair and gallows. It is a commonplace that cruel and hard punishments cannot be inflicted unless the populace is moved by hatred and fear. The psychology of fighting crime is the same as the psychology of fighting wars: the people must be made to hate before they will kill.

After the Chicago Crime Commission's first year in business, the crime rate appeared to decline, and the Commission patted itself on the back. But as soon as the rate climbed back up, the Commission looked for a scapegoat. It blamed soft-hearted judges and misguided social workers, with their "maudlin sympathy" for criminals. The favorite targets of the Commission were probation and parole, the only real advances in penology that had been made in centuries. Calling probation "a vicious measure," the president of the Commission demanded a return to old-fashioned retributive punishment, which had been effective in preserving life and property. "Our fundamental criminal laws are the development of centuries of civilization," the Commission boasted, though it was during these centuries of civilization that a child could be hanged for stealing a loaf of bread or a stick of candy.

Even in the twenties it was customary for the vigilante groups to promote the myth that prisons were "country clubs." The Commission's president wrote: "If we are going to make Chicago a safe place to live in, one of the first things we must do is to provide punishment that punishes, instead of giving criminals a vacation in an institution where they have a better living than if they were free."

IV
State and local criminal justice systems

The following two pieces will discuss the two critical components of local criminal justice systems, the police and the prosecutors. The most visible law enforcement agency in any community is, of course, the police, and their performance essentially determines the degree of public confidence in the criminal justice system as a whole. Thus, the police function is critical to the ability of the establishment to maintain its power, for if police efficiency (and, in flagrant cases, honesty) is seriously questioned, it is conceivable that other, more profound, more embarrassing issues might arise. Police failures may come to be perceived as more general social (or political or legal) failures; thus, despite the rivalries and jealousies within the system, all participants instinctively realize that they must either hang together or hang separately. While the police may not always be the "Thin Blue Line" between civilization and anarchy, as they proudly proclaim, they certainly are the thin blue shield between the public and the establishment. The police drive toward "professionalization" (whose momentum has been building since the 1920's) is an effort both to shed the trappings and the continuing insecurities of partisan political influence upon them and, more importantly, to insulate themselves from public scrutiny and to retain *the* vital power in our organizational world, the power to create and use information (of course, both the F.B.I. and the Drug Enforcement Administration, as we have seen, are masters at the game).

Insofar as the police succeed in shielding their activities from public scrutiny and criticism (an enterprise which of course can never be wholly fulfilled) and in controlling the creation and dissemination of crime information, their autonomy is enhanced. Increased police autonomy can only serve the ultimate goals of the establishment—a monopoly (or, at least, a veto) over all decision making about crime and its control in the society, and a recognition of its legitimacy and authority to shape public perceptions about crime. On the local level, the police are engaged in the dual enterprise of seeking greater control over their activities while soliciting public approbation for their victories over what President Nixon once termed "the criminal forces." In their exposed position, the police constitute a unique group: they are of the establishment, but they are simultaneously subject to public pressures not operative upon their sister agencies.

What the police have not yet achieved—autonomy, credibility, and secrecy—has been attained by the prosecutor's office. The inner workings of that office are virtually unknown to the public. The use of immense investigative and prosecutorial resources against disfavored individuals or groups only occasionally surfaces. His discretionary power not to investigate and not to prosecute (or to terminate prosecutions already commenced) is also barely visible. The most surprising lesson we may learn from Professor Abraham Blumberg's commentary is that the prosecutor's power and "invisibility" extend into the ostensible public forum of the courtroom, scarcely diminished by the necessity of dealing with other actors in the criminal justice system.

The two pieces which follow are pieces united by their common concern with the responses of both the police and the prosecutor to problems of (a) retention of public confidence and (b) fulfillment of their own bureaucratic priorities and needs (which have little to do with the ideal of "Equal Justice Under Law"). As both entities struggle to maintain their positions in the "system" free of meaningful public scrutiny, they are fighting the same battle that taxes the energies of all the agencies of the crime-control establishment. As we shall see, the success of that struggle also involves the continued viability of the establishment itself.

A layman contemplating the problem of crime control

would, most likely, identify the establishment with *local* criminal justice institutions, such as the prosecutors, courts, or police. The tendency is a natural—though misleading— one, for we tend to respond to the closest, most visible participants in the system as if they controlled it. Also, our structural and institutional arrangements for dealing with crime tend to localize that phenomenon and, consequently, to inhibit broad perspectives. But, since local criminal justice institutions are precisely that, *local,* and since they are remarkably diverse from community to community (Professor James Wilson, for instance, has identified at least three basic styles of police behavior), there is no objective evidence to indicate that local elites are an establishment in the sense used in the Introduction.

Yet, the activities of these elites—especially the police and the prosecutors—are essential to an understanding of the effectiveness of the establishment. They are functionaries within the broad outlines of the system perpetuated by the groups of which I have previously spoken. Just as establishment values in the realm of foreign policy are carried into effect and therefore reinforced by State Department employees (the Foreign Service, etc.), so a similar process is operative at the local crime-control level. If a national hysteria about Communism exists and is perpetuated or even created by the F.B.I., it is reinforced by the creation of "Red Squads" within local police departments. If a particular enemy—the drug pusher—is the subject of vehement attack by the Bureau of Narcotics, then state laws and police priorities are harnessed to the requirements of this particular "war." In turn, of course, public attitudes are affected by what becomes a concerted and comprehensive attack on crime. Thus, the role of the functionaries within local criminal justice systems more than merely supports the establishment; it is critical to its ability to function at all. This is so for several reasons. Thus, local crime control provides the necessary manpower and other resources in combined Federal-State crime-fighting efforts. Local sucesses tend to gain public support for *all* crime-control agencies and efforts, and the ties between local law enforcement and local politics tend to spill over, so that locally elected

Congressmen are responsive to pressures for expanded efforts (and more money) to fight crime at all levels.

At the local level, confusion apparently abounds. The public is treated to the spectacle of endless discord among police, judges, prosecutors, and corrections officials. Occasionally, either in public esteem or in bureaucratic infighting, one group or another seems to prevail. In 1966 in New York City, for instance, the police union, the Patrolman's Benevolent Association, shrewdly and successfully attacked the civilian-dominated police review board and convinced the public at large to reject it. Superficially, then, it might seem that a local "police establishment" existed—and, indeed, there were dire prophecies that police unionization would lead to increasing participation by that group in all areas of criminal justice—but, once the Review Board battle had been won, the P.B.A. did not become policy-oriented. In fact, there is still considerable turmoil among the police about the entire subject of unionization, and the ability of the police to achieve their ends has been spotty. It is characteristic of institutions within local criminal justice systems that their interests are parochial and, essentially, defensive—they protect their own turf—though where they manifest (or at least claim) some form of expertise, they may occasionally influence the political process. Often—as in the case of Governor Nelson Rockefeller's controversial drug proposals in New York State in 1972–73—even determined opposition by judges and district attorneys' groups proved to be a dismal failure.

The critical importance, then, of such local groups is their supportive (or satellite) roles within or perhaps peripheral to the establishment. No picture of the establishment could be complete without an understanding of that role. Essentially, they are concerned with the nuts and bolts of the system, with reforms that tinker, that are designed to make the system work better (*i.e.,* more smoothly). These groups neither formulate overall policy on crime and its control nor have much public impact beyond their immediate locales (and then only on certain, often minor issues). Their activities mesh well with ongoing establishment concerns, and they are necessary to the success of the establishment, but their roles must be seen in context. The policeman on the beat has probably as much (unreviewable) discretion in the enforcement of law as does the district attorney deciding whether or not to prosecute or—often more importantly—what to prosecute for. How does the policeman perceive his role? How does a department—as distinguished from the lowest man in the hierarchy—respond to public demands for efficiency, when it cannot by any reasonable standard ever be truly efficient? How should they exercise their discretion, or should they not exercise it at all? Peter K. Manning has attempted to formulate a theory of the police function; while it does not always distinguish among various levels of the police hierarchy, it is a valuable analysis of at least some of the ways in which the police respond to what they believe to be their "impossible mandate."

Abraham Blumberg has been the most vigorous critic of the lower criminal court bureaucracy and its dedication to processing defandants rather than according justice. In recent years, he has been joined by a host of reformers—both hard-line and soft—who also believe that speedy justice is necessary to all participants in the system. There is a certain inconsistency, for speedy justice may well accentuate the bureaucratic tendencies which Blumberg deplores. On the other hand, the nature of his critique is somewhat disparate: at times, one isn't sure whether bureaucracy is being condemned for its own sake, or because it leads to pressures to compel the innocent to plead guilty, or perhaps because it demeans the criminal justice process by giving it the flavor of a bazaar mart (making the defendant more cynical than he already is).

The problem is deeper than Blumberg admits to, for the nature of urban life and our predominant social values have made our criminal justice system the means for dealing with the "rebellious poor." The poor man does not have to walk into an overcrowded urban courtroom to develop his cynicism toward a society which has left him behind. Its facelessness is apparent to him at every turn, and it is doubtful whether the symbol of the adversarial system and Equal Justice has much meaning for him in the first place. This is not to say that the system should not strive to be compassionate and humane, but only that it will not save the society from its benign neglect of the poor. Indeed, Blumberg's only apparent solution is to return to a fullblown adversarial system, with gladiatorial contests at every turn, an impractical proposal and one which might, moreover, not materially raise the standards of Justice—for the defendant, under such circumstances, is often also reduced to being a spectator at his own fate.

The power of the prosecutor in the present system is central, yet surprisingly little has been written about it. He is the focus of what might be called the "establishment satellite system"; he maneuvers the judge, the arresting police officer, and the defendant into accepting the values of the "ongoing" system. Along with the police and the judges, he labors to put the best face on the existing criminal justice institutions, and he performs a key role in gaining public acceptance of establishment values.

His discretion, once crime has been called to his attention, is vast and virtually unreviewable. He chooses any one of, or combination of, an assortment of indictable offenses with which to charge a suspect, virtually controls the grand jury where the indictment is sought (in many states, he may file an "information" and dispense with a grand jury altogether), and has unlimited power to delay, bargain, and control and manage the calendar to his satisfaction.

The only consistent picture we have of the prosecutor is that (offered by Blumberg and Jerome Skolnick, among others) of the harassed, overworked "calendar clearer" and plea bargainer. Yet, we know empirically that young, ambitious attorneys do enter the prosecutor's office to gain trial experience and to eventually follow either lucrative legal, or powerful political, careers. Their aspirations are highly individualistic and driving; yet, we know of them only as bureaucratic nonentities. More careful work must be done to reconcile these contradictory images, for we can assume that certain kinds of cases are not "bargainable" and that the prosecutor may insist upon a trial where publicity, sex crimes, political crimes, and perhaps other types of considerations are present.

chapter six

The policeman as hero

PETER K. MANNING

The policeman judges himself against the ideal policeman as described in police occupational lore and imagery. What a "good policeman" does is an omnipresent standard. The occupational culture, however, contains more than the definition of a good policeman. It contains the typical values, norms, attitudes, and material paraphernalia of an occupational group.

An occupational culture also prompts the *assumptions* about everyday life that become the basis for organizational strategies and tactics. Recent studies of the occupational culture of the police allow the formulation of the following postulates or assumptions, all of which are the basis for police strategies to be discussed later:

1. People cannot be trusted; they are dangerous.
2. Experience is better than abstract rules.
3. You must make people respect you.
4. Everyone hates a cop.
5. The legal system is untrustworthy; policemen make the best decisions about guilt or innocence.
6. People who are not controlled will break laws.
7. Policemen must appear respectable and be efficient.
8. Policemen can most accurately identify crime and criminals.
9. The major jobs of the policeman are to prevent crime and to enforce the laws.
10. Stronger punishment will deter criminals from repeating their errors.

From *The Police*, by Peter K. Manning, in *Crime and Justice in American Society*, ed. by Jack Douglas (Indianapolis: The Bobbs-Merrill Co., 1972). © 1972 by The Bobbs-Merrill Co. Reprinted by permission of the author.

Professor Manning is also the author of the forthcoming book *Police Work*.

Some qualifications about these postulates are in order. They apply primarily to the American noncollege-educated patrolman. They are less applicable to administrators of urban police departments and to members of minority groups within these departments. Nor do they apply accurately to nonurban, state, and federal policemen.

THE "IMPOSSIBLE" MANDATE

The police in modern society are in agreement with their audiences—which include their professional interpreters, the American family, criminals, and politicians—in at least one respect: they have an "impossible" task.

Several rather serious consequences result from the public's image of the police. The public is aware of the dramatic nature of a small portion of police work, but it ascribes the element of excitement to all police activities. To much of the public, the police are seen as alertly ready to respond to citizen demands, as crime-fighters, as an efficient, bureaucratic, highly organized force that keeps society from falling into chaos. The policeman himself considers the essence of his role to be the dangerous and heroic enterprise of crook-catching and the watchful prevention of crimes. The system of positive and negative sanctions from the public and within the department encourages this heroic conception. The public wants crime prevented and controlled; that is, it wants criminals caught. Headlines herald the accomplishments of G-Men and F.B.I. agents who often do catch dangerous men, and the reputation of these federal authorities not infrequently rubs off on local policemen who are much less adept at catching criminals.

In an effort to gain the public's confidence in their ability, and to insure thereby the solidity of their mandate, the police have encouraged the public to continue thinking of them and their work in idealized terms, terms, that is, which grossly exaggerate the actual work done by police. They do engage in chases, in gunfights, in careful sleuthing. But these are rare events. Most police work resembles any other kind of work: it is boring, tiresome, sometimes dirty, sometimes technically demanding, but it is rarely dangerous. Yet the occasional chase, the occasional shoot-out, the occasional triumph of some extraordinary detective work have been seized upon by the police and played up to the public. The public's response has been to demand even more dramatic crook-catching and crime prevention, and this demand for arrests has been converted into an index for measuring how well the police accomplish their mandate. The public's definitions have been converted by the police organization into distorted criteria for promotion, success, and security.

THE PROBLEMATIC NATURE
OF LAW AND ORDER

A society's laws, it is often said, reflect its customs; it can also be said that the growth of the criminal law is proportionate to the decline in the consistency and binding nature of these mores. In simpler societies, where the codes and rules of behavior were well known and homogeneous, sanctions were enforced with much greater uniformity and predictability. Social control was isomorphic with one's obligations to family, clan, and age group, and the political system of the tribe. In a modern, differentiated society, a minimal number of values and norms are shared. And because the fundamental, taken-for-granted consensus on what is proper and respectable has been blurred or shattered, or, indeed, never existed, criminal law becomes a basis of social control.

Social control through the criminal law predominates in a society only when other means of control have failed. When it does predominate, it no longer reflects the mores of the society. It more accurately reflects the interests of shifting power groups within the society.

The perspective of the patrolman as he goes about his daily rounds is a legalistic one. The law and the administrative actions of his department provide him with a frame of reference for exercising the mandate of the police. The citizen, on the other hand, does not live his life in accordance with a legalistic framework; he defines his acts in accordance with a moral or ethical code provided him by his family, his religion, his social class. For the most part, he sees law enforcement as an intervention in his private affairs.

No matter what the basis for actions of private citizens may be, however, the patrolman's job is one of practical decision-making within a legalistic pattern. Wilson summarizes the difficulty inherent in law enforcement as follows:

> Most criminal laws define *acts* (murder, rape, speeding, possessing narcotics), which are held to be illegal; people may disagree as to whether the

act should be illegal, as they do with respect to narcotics, for example, but there is little disagreement as to what the behavior in question consists of. Laws regarding disorderly conduct and the like assert, usually by implication, that there is a condition ("public order") that can be diminished by various actions. The difficulty, of course, is that public order is nowhere defined and can never be defined unambiguously because what constitutes order is a matter of opinion and convention, not a state of nature. (An unmurdered person, an unraped woman, and an unpossessed narcotic can be defined so as to be recognizable to any reasonable person.) An additional difficulty, a corollary of the first, is the impossibility of specifying, except in the extreme case, what degree of disorder is intolerable and who is to be held culpable for that degree. A suburban street is quiet and pleasant; a big city street is noisy and (to some) offensive; what degree of noise and offense, and produced by whom, constitutes "disorderly conduct"? [1]

The complexity of the law and the difficulty in obtaining a complainant combine to tend to make the policeman underenforce the law—to overlook, ignore, dismiss, or otherwise erase the existence of many enforceable breaches of the law.

Some researchers and legalists have begun to piece together a pattern of the conditions under which policemen have a tendency not to enforce the law. From a study of police in three Midwestern states, LaFave has concluded that two considerations characterize a decision not to arrest. The first is that the crime is unlikely to reach public attention—for example, that it is of a private nature or of low visibility—and the second is that underenforcement is unlikely to be detected or challenged.[2] Generally, the conditions under which policemen are less likely to enforce the law are those in which they perceive little public consensus on the law, or in which the law is ambiguous. LaFave found that policemen are not apt to enforce rigorously laws that are viewed by the public as dated, or that are used on the rare occasions when the public order is being threatened.

In the exercise of discretion, in the decision to enforce the law or to underenforce, the protection of individual rights is often at stake. But individual rights are frequently in opposition to the preservation of order, as a totalitarian state exemplifies in the extreme. The police try to manage these two contradictory demands by empha-

---

[1] Wilson, *Varieties of Police Behavior*, pp. 21–22.
[2] LaFave, *Arrest*.

sizing their peace-keeping functions. This emphasis succeeds only when a consensus exists on the nature of the order (peace) to be preserved. The greater the difference in viewpoint between the police and the public on the degree and kind of order to be preserved, the greater will be antagonism between the two; the inevitable result of this hostility will be "law breaking."

The resolution of the contradictions and complexities inherent in the police mandate, including the problems of police discretion, of individual rights, of law enforcement and peace-keeping, is not helped, however, by the involvement of police in politics. Politics only further complicates the police mandate. The law itself is a political phenomenon, and at the practical level of enforcing it, the local political system is yet another source of confusion.

THE POLICE IN THE POLITICAL SYSTEM

[There] is [a] massive dispersal of police authority—and political authority—throughout the nation . . . with overlapping laws governing law enforcement. [Thus, it is clear that] the responsibility for maintaining public order in America is decentralized, and that law-enforcement officers are largely under the immediate control of local political authorities.

The second reason why the police are an integral part of the political system is this: law is a political entity, and the administration of criminal law unavoidably encompasses political values and political ends. The police are directly related to a political system that develops and defines the law, itself a product of interpretations of what is right and proper from the perspective of different politically powerful segments within the community.

The third reason why the police are tied to the political system emanates from the second: the police must administer the law. Many factors pattern this enforcement, but they all reflect the political organization of society. The distribution of power and authority, for example, rather than the striving for justice, or equal treatment under the law, can have a direct bearing on enforcement.

There are several direct effects of the political nature of the police mandate. One is that many policemen become alienated; they lose interest in their role as enforcers and in the law as a believable criterion. The pressures of politics also erode loyalty to the police organization and not infrequently lead to collusion with criminals and organized crime.

The policeman's exposure to danger, his social background, low pay, low morale, his vulnerability in a repressive bureaucracy all conspire to make him susceptible to the lures of the underhanded and the appeals of the political. Studies reveal a political profile of the policeman as a conservative, perhaps reactionary, person of lower-class or lower-middle-class origin, often a supporter of radical right causes, often prejudiced and repressive, often extremely ambivalent about the rights of others. The postulates or assumptions of the police culture, the suspiciousness, fear, low self-esteem, and distrust of others are almost diametrically opposed to the usual conception of the desirable democratic man.

Thus, the enforcement of some laws is personally distasteful. Civil-rights legislation, for example, can be anathema. Or truculence can be the reaction to an order relaxing controls in ghettos during the summer months. It is the ambivalence of policemen toward certain laws and toward certain local policies that fragments loyalty within a department and causes alienation.

Police and politics within the community are tightly interlocked. The sensitivity of the police to their political audiences, their operation within the political system of criminal justice, and their own personal political attitudes undermine their efforts to fulfill their contradictory mandate and to appear politically neutral.

THE EFFICIENT, SYMPTOM-ORIENTED ORGANIZATION

The Wickersham report, the Hoover administration's report on crime and law enforcement in the United States, was published in 1931. This precursor of the Johnson administration's *The Challenge of Crime in a Free Society* became a rallying point for advocates of police reform. One of its central themes was the lack of "professionalism" among the police of the time—their lack of special training, their corruption, their brutality, and their use of illegal procedures in law enforcement. And one of its results was that the police, partly in order to demonstrate their concern with scientific data gathering on crime and partly to indicate their capacity to "control" crime itself, began to stress crime statistics as a major component of professional police work.

Crime statistics, therefore—and let this point be emphasized—became a police construction. The actual amount of crime committed in a society is unknown—and probably unknowable, given the private nature of most crime. The *crime rate,* consequently, is simply a construction of police activities. That is, the crime rate pertains only to "crimes known to the police," crimes that have been reported to or observed by the police and for which adequate grounds exist for assuming that a violation of the law has, in fact, taken place. (The difference between the *actual* and *known crimes* is often called the "dark figure of crime.") Of course, the construction of a crime rate placed the police in a logically weak position in which they still find themselves. If the crime rate is rising, they argue that more police support is needed to fight the war against crime; if the crime rate is stable or declining, they argue that they have successfully combated the crime menace—a heads-I-win-tails-you-lose proposition.

In spite of their inability to control the commission of illegal acts (roughly, the actual rate), since they do not know about all crime, the police have claimed responsibility for crime control, using the crime rate as an index of their success. This use of the crime rate to measure success is somewhat analogous to their use of a patrolman's arrest rate as an indication of his personal success in law enforcement. Questions about the actual amount of crime and the degree of control exercised are thus bypassed in favor of an index that offers great potential for organizational or bureaucratic control. Instead of grappling with the difficult issue of defining the ends of police work and an operational means for accomplishing them, the police have opted for "efficient" law-enforcement defined in terms of fluctuations of the crime rate. They have transformed concern with undefined ends into concern with available means. Their inability to cope with the causes of crime—which might offer them a basis for defining their ends—shifts their "organizational focus" into symptomatic concerns, that is, into a preoccupation with the rate of crime, not its reasons.

This preoccupation with the symptoms of a problem rather than with the problem itself is typical of all bureaucracies. For one characteristic of a bureaucracy is goal-displacement. Bureaucratic organizations tend to lose track of their goals and engage in ritual behavior, substituting means for ends. As a whole, bureaucracies become so engrossed in pursuing, defending, reacting to, and, even, in creating immediate problems that their objective is forgotten. This tendency to displace goals is accelerated by the one value dear to all bureaucracies—efficiency. Efficiency is the be-all and end-all of bureaucratic organizations. Thus, they can expend great effort without any genuine accomplishment.

MAJOR STRATEGIES OF THE POLICE

Rather than resolving their dilemmas, the police have manipulated them with a professional eye on just how well the public accepts their dexterity. Thus, law enforcement becomes a self-justifying system. It becomes more responsive to its own needs, goals, and procedures than to serving society. In this section, we will show the ways in which the police have followed the course of most other bureaucratic institutions in society, responding to their problems by merely giving the appearance of facing them while simultaneously promoting the trained incapacity to do otherwise.

The two primary aims of most bureaucracies, the police included, are the maintenance of their organizational autonomy and the security of their members. To accomplish these aims, they adopt a pattern of institutional action that can best be described as "professionalism." This word, with its many connotations and definitions, cloaks all the many kinds of actions carried out by the police.

The guise of professionalism embodied in a bureaucratic organization is the most important strategy employed by the police to defend their mandate and thereby to build self-esteem, organizational autonomy, and occupational solidarity or cohesiveness. The professionalization drives of the police are no more suspect than the campaigns of other striving, upwardly mobile occupational groups. However, since the police have a monopoly on legal violence, since they are the active enforcers of the public will, serving theoretically in the best interests of the public, the consequences of their yearnings for prestige and power are imbued with far greater social ramifications than the relatively harmless attempts of florists, funeral directors, and accountants to attain public stature.

Disinterested law enforcement through bureaucratic means is an essential in our society and in any democracy, and the American police are certainly closer to attaining this ideal than they were in 1931 at the time of the Wickersham report. Professionalism qua professionalism is unquestionably desirable in the police. But if in striving for the heights of prestige they fail to serve the altruistic values of professionalism, if their professionalism means that a faulty portrait of the social reality of crime is being painted, if their professionalism conceals more than it reveals about the true nature of their operations, then a close analysis of police professionalism is in order.

Police professionalism cannot be easily separated in practice from the bureaucratic ideal epitomized in modern police practice. The bureaucratic ideal is established as a means of obtaining a commitment from personnel to organizational and occupational norms. This bureaucratic commitment is designed to supersede commitments to competing norms, such as obligations to friends or kin or members of the same racial or ethnic group. Unlike medicine and law, professions that developed outside the context of bureaucracies, policing has always been carried out, if done on a full-time basis, as a bureaucratic function.

Modern police bureaucracy and modern police professionalism are highly articulated, although they contain some inherent stresses that are not our present concern. The strategies employed by the police to manage their public appearance develop from their adaptation of the bureaucratic ideal. These strategies incorporate the utilization of *technology* and *official statistics* in law enforcement, of *styles of patrol* that attempt to accommodate the community's desire for public order with the police department's preoccupation with bureaucratic procedures, of *secrecy* as a means of controlling the public's response to their operations, of *collaboration* with criminal elements to foster the appearance of a smoothly run, law-abiding community, and of a *symbiotic relationship* with the criminal justice system that minimizes public knowledge of the flaws within this largely privately operated system.

PROFESSIONALISM

To say that a type of work can only be carried out by professionals is to make both it and them immediately acceptable.

The need of the police to proclaim themselves professionals arises out of their need to control both the public and their own organization. Internally, professionalism functions to unify the diverse interests and elements that exist within any occupational or organizational group. This view sees professionalism as an ideology. Habenstein has described it as follows:

> Certain groups, claiming special functions, have been able to arrogate to themselves, or command increased power over, the conditions of members' livelihood. . . . "Profession" is, basically, an ideology, a set of rationalizations about the worth and necessity of certain areas of work, which, when internalized, gives the practitioners a moral justification for privilege, if not license. . . .[3]

Efforts toward the professionalization of any occupation are, above all, efforts to achieve power and authority. In police work, professionalization serves the self-esteem of all practitioners, from patrolman to commissioner, by gilding the entire enterprise with the symbols, prerequisites, tradition, power, and authority of the most respected occupations in American society.

THE BUREAUCRATIC IDEAL

The organizational *ideal* of the "professional" police department is a rational, efficient, scientifically organized, technologically sophisticated bureaucracy. To them, a bureaucracy is the best device for managing appearances and the best method of working out a running adjustment to the pressing nature of their problems. And bureaucratic rhetoric, with its reverence for science and professionalism, is accurately assessed as the most powerful source of legitimation in American society.

TECHNOLOGY

One of the strategies employed by the police to appear professional and bureaucratically efficient is the use of technology. [Scien-

[3] Robert W. Habenstein, "Critique of 'Profession' as a Sociological Category." *Sociological Quarterly* 4 (November 1963), p. 297. This notion follows H. S. Becker's in "The Nature of a Profession," in *Yearbook of the National Society for the Study of Education* (Chicago: National Society for the Study of Education, 1961).

tific] devices illustrate the technological strategy and are related to the police asumptions that if they have more information more quickly, more visibility, more policemen, more firepower, and better allocation of resources, all organized around technology, they will be able to efficiently prevent and deter crime. These assumptions are also manifested in the President's crime commission report. The police have brought a scientific perspective to crime prevention, elaborating on the means of obtaining more information more quickly, and on methods of more efficiently allocating men, material, and more potent weapons. Technology, of course, does not deal with the great difficulties in obtaining information.

OFFICIAL STATISTICS

The police construct and utilize official statistics, such as the clearance rate and the crime index, to manage the impression of efficiency. The clearance rate, so popular among professionalized police departments, is a measure of a patrolman's or a detective's efficiency. Offenses categorized as "solved" become part of the clearance rate. The police ignore all unreported crimes and all crimes without victims where no complainant is required; these crimes, therefore, are never "cleared"—they never become part of the clearance rate. As for the index of crime being an index of efficiency, no mandatory, centralized crime-reporting system exists, although many police departments have adopted and report on the basis of the F.B.I. index of crimes: murder, aggravated assault, rape, burglary, robbery, larceny over $50, and auto theft. Needless to say, the more the police enforce the laws, the higher the crime rate. Because there has been very little in the way of standard reporting and investigation practices, the police have been able to control the crime rate to a large degree by controlling aspects of enforcement.

STYLES OF PATROL

The tasks absorbed by the police have burgeoned in recent years—along with the demands for their services. The police have tried to answer these demands of their environment by three distinct types of patrol—what Wilson describes as the *watchman,*

legalistic, and *service* styles.[4] The watchman style is the classic mode
of policing urban areas and is still used in some degree in most
cities. It is a style of patrol that emphasizes maintenance of public
order rather than enforcement of the law. The policeman is instructed to be sensitive to the interests of groups within his beat
and to overlook many of the minor offenses connected with juvenile
infractions, traffic violations, vice, and gambling. A legalistic style,
on the other hand, rests heavily upon enforcement of the law to
control the routine situations encountered by the patrolman. The
police using this style of patrol are instructed to act as if a single
level of order was desirable in all settings and for all groups, and
to enforce the law to that end. The service style, Wilson's third
type of patrol, is "market-oriented," that is, it is designed to meet
the fairly well-articulated demand of "homogeneous middle-class
communities." The police respond to and take seriously all calls
for police action (unlike the watchman style which ignores certain
kinds of demands for intervention), but (unlike the legalistic style
which it more closely resembles) the police seldom use the law to
control the situation. They prefer informal action to law enforcement.

The value of these varied styles to the police is the survival
potential they provide. They allow the police administrator a certain leeway in trying to control his men in line with the demands
of the most powerful interests in the community and to mitigate
the strain between preserving individual liberty and protecting
the collective social enterprise.

SECRECY AND PUBLIC COMPLAINTS

No matter what the level of operation of a police force, it
will generate citizen complaints. It will generate complaints because the role of the policeman is to restrain and control, not to
advise and remedy. While advice and solutions are usually wel-
come, restraint is not. For a substantial proportion of the population, the policeman is an adversary; he issues summonses, makes
arrests, conducts inquiries, searches homes and people, stops cars,
testifies in court, and keeps a jail. For the police, threats from
outside, such as citizens' complaints and political moves to control

[4] Wilson, *Varieties of Police Behavior,* pp. 140–141.

police policy, are efforts to destroy their organization. One strategy used by police to withstand these threats is to keep all information they obtain secret.

The shared secrets possessed by the police assist them in creating internal cohesion. Information is concealed for the additional reason that the police fear and dislike their clients—the various segments of the public. Westley, one of the first and most profound sociological analysts of the police culture, here describes the occupational perspective of the policeman and the centrality of secrecy:

> The policeman finds his most pressing problems in his relationships to the public. His is a service occupation but of an incongruous kind, since he must discipline those whom he serves. He is regarded as corrupt and inefficient by, and meets with hostility and criticism from, the public. He regards the public as his enemy, feels his occupation to be in conflict with the community, and regards himself to be a pariah. The experience and the feeling give rise to a collective emphasis on secrecy, an attempt to coerce respect from the public, and a belief that almost any means are legitimate in completing an important arrest. These are for the policeman basic occupational values. They arise from his experience, take precedence over his legal responsibilities, [and] are central to an understanding of his conduct. . . .[5]

One aspect of the secrecy strategy is that it constrains many citizens from making complaints about police misconduct. No adequate records are kept on police malfeasance. While the misconduct of the citizen—his law-breaking activities—are closely monitored and recorded, little attempt is made by most departments to maintain publicly available records of police wrongdoing. Certainly, few cities have bureaus that make systematic examinations of police activities for public assessment. Many efforts by citizens to set up public files on police services or to create civilian review boards have failed. The police have in every instance opposed moves to establish evaluational mechanisms; they have continued to prefer losing most citizens' complaints in an endless tangle of red tape. The battle with crime thus goes on largely unmonitored by the public at large.

One solution to corruption is said to be better educated, more professional policemen. By recruiting better educated men, the more professionalized police departments also seek to diminish

---

[5] Westley, "Violence and the Police," p. 35.

the expression of political attitudes on the job and the tendency
of policemen to form political power groups based on their occupation. These are also assumptions made by the crime commission's task force on police. There is, however, no evidence that
college-educated or better-paid policemen are "better policemen";
nor is there any evidence that "better men" alone will solve the
essentially structural problems of the occupation.

SYMBIOSIS AND JUSTICE

Although the police have the principal discretion in the
field with reference to the detection, surveillance, and appraisal of
alleged offenders, the final disposition of a criminal case must be
made in the courts. The police are thus dependent on the courts
in a very special way for their successes. The ideal model of the
criminal-justice system makes the police essentially the fact gatherers
and apprehenders, while the courts are to be the decision-makers.

The police attempt to appear efficient has led them, as we have
noted before, to seek the good pinch, the arrest that will stand up
in court. With victimless crimes, such as those involving gambling
or drugs or prostitution, the police control the situation since they
alone decide whether an offense has been committed and whether
they have a legal case against the offender. To control the success
rate in these cases, the police create a gaggle of informants, many
of whom are compelled to give the police evidence in order to stay
free of a potential charge against themselves for a violation similar
to the one they are providing information about. In the case of
more serious crimes, the problems are more complex; in these cases
the police must rely on other informants, and their discretion on
arrests and charges are more often exercised by administrators and
prosecuting attorneys.

There are several undesirable effects of this symbiosis. It encourages corruption by permitting the police to make decisions
about the freedom of their informants; it gives them an illegal
hold and power over them, and thus it undercuts the rule of law.

CONCLUSIONS AND PROPOSED
REFORMS

The policeman's view of his role and his occupational culture are very influential in determining the nature of policing.

The basic source of police trouble is the inability of the police to define a mandate that will minimize the inconsistent nature of their self-expectations and the expectations of those they serve.

The problems derived from a contradictory mandate remain unaffected by the efforts of the institution to solve them; they do, however, take the shape into which they have been cast by institutional functionaries. Cooley long ago discussed the process of institutional ossification, the process by which institutions stray from serving the needs of their members and their publics, thereby losing the loyalty of those within and the support of those without. The consequences of institutional ossification as related to the police are twofold. First, the police begin to search for a so-called higher order of legitimacy; they make appeals to morality, to patriotism, to "Americanism," and to "law and order" to shore up eroded institutional charters and to accelerate their attempts to control and manipulate their members and clients. Second, the police, as they develop a far greater potential for controlling those they serve through their presentational strategies, come to serve themselves better than ever before.

The problem of the police is, essentially, the problem of the democratic society, and until the central values and social structures of our society are modified (and I think we are seeing such a modification), there can be no real change in the operation of social control.

Changes in laws to reduce their absolutistic element and to free people who deviate with little harm to others from the onus of criminalization cannot be accomplished without a parallel change in the nature of police accountability. As we have seen, the strategies of secrecy and rhetoric used by the police play on the fears of society and provide a basis for police control. Urgently required are specific ways in which the cities can control the police and make them strictly accountable for their actions—methods, that is, which go a good deal further than merely disposing of the chief or convening a judicial review board. To give city governments this kind of control over the police, however, entails the reorganization of police departments themselves so that their goals are clear and defined and so that the occupational rewards within the police organization are aligned with public goals.

Three interrelated organizational changes must be made to insure that police attend to the job of maintaining public order.

One is to reorganize police departments along functional lines aimed at peace-keeping rather than law enforcement; the second is to allocate rewards for keeping the peace rather than for enforcing the law; the third is to decentralize police functions to reflect community control without the diffusion of responsibility and accountability to a central headquarters.

Present police departments are organized in a military fashion; orders move down the line from the chief to departmental sections assigned law-enforcement functions. These sections usually include such divisions as traffic, patrol, records, detective, juvenile, intelligence, crime-lab, and communications. The principal basis for the assignment of functions, however, is law enforcement;[6] what is needed is a new set of organizational premises so that the basis for the assignment of functions is not law enforcement but the maintenance of order. As Wilson explains:

> If order were the central mission of the department, there might be a "family disturbance squad," a "drunk and derelict squad," a "riot control squad," and a "juvenile squad"; law enforcement matters would be left to a "felony squad." Instead, there is a detective division organized, in the larger departments, into units specializing in homicide, burglary, auto theft, narcotics, vice, robbery, and the like. The undifferentiated patrol division gets everything else. Only juveniles tend to be treated by specialized units under both schemes, partly because the law requires or encourages such specialization. The law enforcement orientation of most departments means that new specialized units are created for every offense about which the public expresses concern or for which some special technology is required.[7]

What is called for, then, is a new organizational pattern that will provide a domestic unit (as is now being tried in New York City), a juvenile unit, and a drunk unit with a detoxification center, all with a peace-keeping orientation and peace-keeping functions. Only a felony squad and perhaps a riot squad should be used to enforce the law.

One of the obvious ways in which to improve the morale of the patrolman is to let him do a greater amount of investigative work and to take on the responsibility for "solving" some of the crimes originating with his patrol. Rewards could then be allocated in

---

[6] President's Commission, *Task Force Report: The Police,* charts on pp. 46–47.
[7] Wilson, *Varieties of Police Behavior,* p. 69.

accord with the more limited ends of peace-keeping—for instance, in rewarding a patrolman for a decline in the number of drunks who reappear in court. Since no comprehensive policy can be imagined to guide order maintenance, limited ends for various departments must be developed and subjected to public review. The key is to allow the policeman to develop judgment about the motives and future intentions of people with whom he comes in contact, and to reward him for peace-keeping, not "good pinches" alone.

This reappraisal of the allocation of rewards means, of course, that there must be greater coordination of police and other agencies within the criminal-justice system in order to increase the benefits to the client (the offender or the criminal) and break down the isolation of the police. To allow the policeman to assume greater peace-keeping responsibilities would allow him to play a functional role parallel to that of the better general practitioner of medicine: the referral specialist, the coordinator of family health, the source of records and information, and the family friend and counselor. Such an organizational change in the policeman's function would, naturally enough, make community control of the police a greater possibility. It would begin to bridge the chasm between the police and many hostile segments within the public, a process that could be facilitated by the creation of a community-relations division within police departments.

The third needed modification of the present structure of police work is the development of decentralized operations. One of the major social trends of the last ten years has been the increase in the lack of attachment people have for their major institutions. Police today suffer from a crisis of legitimacy, and this crisis is heightened by their failure to promote a sense of commitment to their operations by the citizens they serve. One way in which to introduce commitment and a sense of control over the police by members of a community is to make the police more accessible. St. Louis, for example, has experimented with "storefront" police stations, staffed by a few men who are available as advisers, counselors, protectors, and friends of the people in the immediate neighborhood. If the police should begin to differentiate the role of the patrolman to include the functions of a peace-keeping community agent, the control of these agents should reside in the community. Thus, public participation in the decision-making processes of the police would begin at the precinct or neighborhood level; it would not be simply in the form of a punitive civilian review board or a token citizen board at headquarters.

We began with the notion of trouble, police trouble, the troublesome mandate of the policeman. There will be little succor for him as long as our social structure remains fraught with contradictory value premises, with fragmented political power and the consequent inadequate control of the police, with the transformation of public trusts into institutional rights. There will be little succor for him as long as our political agencies resist moving to de-moralize our criminal laws. As it is, we can expect that the management of crime through police strategies and appearances will continue to be a disruptive element in American society.

c h a p t e r   s e v e n

Due process and
assembly-line justice

ABRAHAM S. BLUMBERG

The rational-instrumental goals of the court organization, in its urgent demand for guilty pleas, have produced a bargain-counter, assembly-line system of criminal justice which is incompatible with traditional due process. The dilemma is sharpened by the fact that the concern for the individual envisioned and postulated by the rules of due process in determining guilt or innocence, is no longer present at this crucial level. Instead, the concern, if any, appears at the post-guilt, pre-sentence stage, while the actual determination of guilt is arrived at through perfunctory ministerial procedures which have become the hallmark of the criminal court's rationality.

The dilemma and its implications may be seen in still another way: the concepts of "due process" and "rule of law" are frequently used interchangeably and have assumed the quality of ritual affirmations. They now have a distinct ideological character in that they distort or conceal some aspect of social reality. Their abstruse, mystical, and protean qualities have helped to obscure the emergence and institutionalization of bureaucratic due process, culminating in a state of affairs in which the overwhelming majority of defendants now plead guilty before trial. What passes for a full, fair, and open "hearing" are the secret negotiation sessions which become forever submerged in the final plea of guilty and are therefore rarely subject to routine examination or review.

The rule of law is not self-executing. It is translated into reality

From *Criminal Justice,* by Abraham S. Blumberg (New York: Quandrangle/ The New York Times Book Company, 1967). © 1967, 1970 by Abraham S. Blumberg. Reprinted by permission of the publisher.

by men in institutions. Traditional constitutional elements of criminal law, when placed in the institutional setting of a modern criminal court, are reshaped by a bureaucratic organization to serve its requirements and goals. In pursuit of production and efficiency, the criminal court's formal and informal organizations have harnessed the court's ideology, structure, and personnel to overcome and alter the rules and safeguards of constitutional due process. The vague and constantly shifting constitutional requirements of due process have allowed the rational, impersonal, and ruthless criteria of modern organizational life to gain primacy, so that the individual accused is minimized and given short shrift. The void created by the historical obscurities and indefiniteness of due process has been filled with definitions that are favorable and peculiar to the bureaucratic world-view, its felt necessities, values, and priorities. The "adversary system" and the "presumption of innocence" are compromised in the framework of the formal court process itself. They are supplanted by a non-adversary, accusatory system which actually favors a presumption of guilt.

Three relatively recent items reported in the *New York Times* underscore this aspect of the matter as it has manifested itself in one of the major criminal courts. In one instance the Bronx County Bar Association condemned "mass assembly-line justice," which was rushing defendants into pleas of guilty and into convictions "in violation of their legal rights." Another item reports the unusual event of a judge criticizing his own court system (the New York Criminal Court) to the effect that "pressure to set statistical records in disposing of cases had hurt the administration of justice." A third, a most unusual recent public discussion in the press in this regard, was a statement by a leading New York appellate judge decrying "instant justice" which is employed to reduce court calendar congestion, "converting our courthouses into counting houses . . . as in most big cities where the volume of business tends to overpower court facilities."

To presume that "law" and "justice" are instruments possible only in certain kinds of societies (i.e., "democratic") is a fanciful oversimplification. Modern totalitarian societies, the ancient despotisms, modern democratic states—all have produced comprehensive juridical systems dispensing "justice." Rome was certainly a model of tyranny in antiquity, and it articulated a legal system which serves as the point of origin of many legal systems today.

The Russia that emerged after the violent upheaval of 1917 thought it could then uproot and dispose of "capitalist law." But such early hopes were soon dashed on the granite realities of the felt necessities for some sort of legal code to regulate all aspects of conduct of the "soviet man" who was to emerge. Terror, naked force, and law merged to deal with "deviationists" and "counter-revolutionary crimes." In the Soviet legal system, law, especially the criminal law, serves as a form of consciousness. It is an instrument of the party in its effort to fashion the Soviet people into loyal, industrious citizens, respectful of the authority of the communist social order.

Raul Hilberg carefully documents the use of the German juridical and bureaucratic apparatus by the Nazis to annihilate methodically a segment of humanity. Existing legal machinery, including the civil and criminal courts, was employed to effect three phases of the destruction process: definition, expropriation, and concentration of the Jews. The first phase dealt with the legal establishment of the answer to the question, "Who is a Jew?" and the judicial determination of all the legal consequences of such status for employment, marriage, and other individual rights and relationships. The second phase concerned itself with the legal and judicial procedures employed in stripping those who had been legally determined to be Jews of most of their property, including jobs, contracts, business enterprises, and personal wealth. The final step provided for the social isolation of the Jews through their total ghettoization by law, the legally compulsory termination of social relations between Jews and others, including elaborate laws relating to intermarriage, housing restrictions, regulations of their movement, and identification procedures. All these measures included severe criminal penalties for violators.

Juridical systems, then, embody and personify particular interpretations of the collective conscience of a social order. The legal concept of due process serves much the same function in the legal system as does the joker in a card game: it has a shifting meaning and application. The structure of legal and juridical systems are a reflection of group structure and the individuals who comprise it. In a rational-legal society, the "rule of law" is invoked as the source of legitimacy. In dealing with a wrongdoer, the question is not guilt or innocence but rather a demonstration of the "approved way" in which violence can be used legitimately vis-à-vis a given

120   *Abraham S. Blumberg*

individual. In American society the "approved way" means due process of law, which in essence refers to the normatively established, institutionalized recipes for invoking and using legal machinery.

Even under optimal circumstances a criminal case is very much a one-sided affair, the parties to the contest being decidedly unequal in strength and resources. But the concern with better and more extensive rules has served as a façade of moral philosophy to divert our gaze from the more significant development of the emergence of "bureaucratic due process," a non-adversary system of justice by negotiation. It consists of secret bargaining sessions, employing subtle, bureaucratically ordained modes of coercion and influence to dispose of onerously large case loads in an efficacious and "rational" manner.

THE CRIMINAL PROCESS: IDEOLOGIES, PRINCIPLES, AND PRACTICES

Society tries to develop social, legal, and organizational structures which will filter out law violators and at the same time provide an avenue of possible freedom to those who are innocent or simply casual law-breakers. The problems posed by the dilemma

TABLE 1. CONVICTION RATES IN CASES DISPOSED OF BY TRIAL IN METROPOLITAN COURT (1950–1964)

Year	Total Cases Disposed of by Trial	Convictions, Number and Per Cent		Acquittals	Disagreements (Hung Juries)
1950	113	92	(81.41)	21	15
1951	137	103	(75.18)	34	12
1952	127	95	(74.80)	32	22
1953	131	101	(77.09)	30	18
1954	112	88	(78.57)	24	8
1955	102	82	(80.39)	20	7
1956	114	94	(82.45)	20	11
1957	115	81	(70.43)	34	8
1958	107	90	(84.11)	17	8
1959	104	96	(92.30)	8	21
1960	116	104	(89.65)	12	6
1961	142	127	(89.43)	15	9
1962	162	142	(87.65)	20	8
1963	150	127	(84.66)	17	6
1964	145	123	(84.82)	14	8

are exacerbated by a society's stated ideological commitments, on the one hand, and by the politics and competing interests of those involved in the system of administering the criminal law, on the other.

THE ROLE OF IDEOLOGY

How then can the court's functionaries and the clients it serves continue to defend as legitimate such a negatively evaluated, oppressive social arrangement? Partly the answer lies in the concept of ideology—the fact that "man does not live by bread alone," that he must seek to develop an ideology to justify, reinforce, and give meaning to interests he pursues. These ideologies and their elaborate rationales become as real and consequential as the material interests. Ideologies need not be and often are not the weapons of a conspiracy of rulers to keep the ruled submerged or to falsify a given state of affairs. On the contrary, they are often nurtured and subscribed to by all strata, rulers and ruled alike, to resolve the inevitable discordancies and incompatibilities of belief systems and behavior or action systems.

There is the almost universal belief on the part of accusers and accused alike in two other basic suppositions:

(1) A defendant in a criminal court is really beaten by the deprivations and limitations imposed by his social class, race, and ethnicity. These in turn preclude such services as bail, legal counsel, psychiatric services, expert witnesses, and investigatory assistance. In essence, the concomitants of poverty are responsible for the fact that due process sometimes produces greatly disparate results in an ill-matched struggle. Further, if these disabilities of the accused were alleviated, then the traditional principles of due process would function to make "justice" available to all. Due process is revered and believed in as the normatively established, time-honored means for obtaining justice, but its lack of vitality is explained away by sociological inequities.

Largely ignored in this argument is the institutional structure— the organizational characteristics and requirements of the criminal court itself. It mediates between the rules as they have been elaborated and the accused person, who has been presented to the court for disposition by still other organizational structures—the police and the district attorney.

The organizational variable affects the values and ideals of normatively established procedures of due process and produces outcomes other than those intended. The *élan vital* of the organization itself has a thrust, purpose, and direction of its own, at variance too often with the stated values of due process. We can tentatively state at least four elements in the organizational variable which tend to deflect it from its prescribed goals:

(a) Occupational and career commitments and drives generate priorities which have a higher claim than the stated organizational goals.

(b) Empire building.

(c) Organizational goals of maximum production, which in their implementation are inconsistent with due process and rule of law.

(d) Institutionalized evasions of due process requirements.

(2) The second basic ideological rationale which supports the legitimacy of the criminal court is the ameliorative-therapeutic model of the court, the origin of which is to be found in the Positivist school of criminology and serves to cast the criminal in the role of a "sick" person. The court then becomes something more than a legal structure; it is also a clinical way station in the long process of individualization of "treatment" of offenders.

For judges, lawyers, probation personnel, and accused persons, the psychiatrist not only has a place in the court setting but tends to validate legal judgments in terms of medical "science." In fact, psychiatry becomes the theology by which legal procedures and pronouncements are interpreted and their legitimacy reinforced for all of the foregoing categories of persons, the accusers and the accused alike. In addition, the charismatic quality of the various occupational roles, even as routinized in the court setting, tends to overwhelm the court's clients, who continue to believe sufficiently in the efficacy, justification, and intentions of psychiatry, probation, and law as "helping" disciplines.

Positivist criminology simply rejects a legal definition of crime and postulates the idea that "punishment" should be replaced by "scientific treatment" of crime. Almost from its inception as a special discipline in medicine, psychiatry has had a role in the administration of the criminal law. As psychiatry developed its theories and made contributions to the study of human behavior, especially in the deviant and the criminal, it also became more powerful socially and politically. Psychiatry has greatly affected the ideas of those who deal with offenders administratively in courts and prisons—as well as in the more remote sphere of human organization in the corporation, shop, factory, and office. Every bureaucracy now has a psychiatric practitioner on tap to deal with the maverick or cantankerous employee—or for that matter anyone —who appears to have "gotten out of line."

But the connection between psychiatry and the court's ameliorative-therapeutic concept is best understood in terms of psychiatry's objectives. Basic to psychiatry as an intellectual effort is its attempt to understand the nature of human behavior and its development, and to control its direction and purpose by manipulating the individual and his environment. Psychiatry, through research and evaluation, claims to develop indices of predictability about human conduct, making possible controlled results for the greater felicity of man and society. But instead, psychiatry, through what one of its most distinguished practitioners in the criminal courts has termed its "psychoauthoritarianism," has become in many instances a *threat* to offenders, because psychiatrists are called upon to participate in virtually every stage of a criminal proceeding. As a consequence, that which another prominent authority in the field, in an unflattering comparison with wire tapping, has termed "mind tapping," is employed without the consent or cooperation of the accused. The practical effect is often to deprive him of certain elements of due process, including the privilege against self-incrimination or ultimately even the right to a trial. For once a psychiatrist has determined that a person is "mentally ill" or "sick" and unable to stand trial, he is more than likely to spend a much longer time behind bars in a mental hospital than if he had been simply convicted of a crime in the first place.

The nosologies, the jargon, and the values of psychiatry, as they are embodied in the ameliorative-therapeutic model which is used in the criminal court, help to disguise and falsify the reality of what occurs. The most analogous situation is the custodial-mental hospital setting, where what is for all practical purposes a prison, presents a therapeutic façade.

The heart of the matter, however, is that in its relationship with other institutions, publics, and its clients, the court uses the language of therapy to justify such varied phenomena as the juvenile court, the indeterminate sentence, the sexual offender laws and civil commitment of the mentally ill, and the use of psychiatric reports before guilt or innocence is determined. Even judges speak the language when imposing sentence.

In practice, measures and techniques that tend to deprive a person of liberty under the guise of an exercise in therapeutic method are seen as punishment, and psychiatry has been seriously criticized on that account. The most strenuous objectors have indicated, in effect, that psychiatry has lent itself to questionable enterprises, and its affirmations of helping through punishment virtually amounts to the discipline being unable to perceive the real nature of its role.

Metropolitan Court has in fact reached the ideal-typical goal in personnel and structure. In its arrangements for bail, counsel, and elaborate psychiatric and probation services, it represents what all who have had serious concern with the criminal court have hoped for. But the court which serves as the universe of this case study produces an administrative result in which the overwhelming majority of defendants simply plead guilty. The idealized version of due process is not translated into social action. The administrative instruments and resources are co-opted in behalf of the court organization to deal more effectively with a large caseload of defendants, by processing them toward a guilty plea.

INSTRUMENTS AND PRESSURES
PROMOTING PLEAS OF GUILTY

The fundamental event which places an accused upon the horns of a dilemma, leading to his ultimate desire for a negotiated or bargained lesser plea, is very simply the decline of the jury system. Whatever that system's merits or drawbacks may be, the fact is that defendants shun a jury trial. The individual accused knows (whether he senses it intuitively or has learned it from his jail companions or his lawyer) that juries are notoriously prone to convict. In simple terms, the outcome of any jury trial often turns upon the question of whom the jury will believe—the assertions of the police, law enforcement officials and their witnesses, or the accused. The answer forthcoming with frequent regularity is: the police and those offering testimony in their behalf. This fact lies at the root of an accused's reluctance to risk a jury trial and in part accounts for the consequent decline of the jury as an important feature of the system.

An indictment is a list of criminal charges. Its purpose is to notify an accused of the precise nature of his alleged offenses so that he may prepare a defense. But a law violation which occurs through a single act can legally result in one being charged with several offenses. A typical indictment for, let us say, possession of more than an eighth of an ounce of heroin, will read as follows:

Count #1. Felonious possession of a narcotic drug.
Count #2. Felonious possession of a narcotic drug with intent to sell.
Count #3. Unlawfully possessing a narcotic drug.

A quite common indictment for burglary may read:
Count #1. Burglary 3rd degree.
Count #2. Possession of burglar's instruments.
Count #3. Unlawful entry of a building.

Or one for armed robbery:
Count #1. Robbery 1st degree.
Count #2. Assault 2nd degree.
Count #3. Assault 3rd degree.
Count #4. Grand larceny 1st degree.
Count #5. Carrying a dangerous weapon.
Count #6. Petit larceny.

The pressure on the accused to seek some sort of compromise of all these charges becomes intense, to say the least. Conviction by a jury on all counts could result in an accused spending the rest of his life in prison.

There are, therefore, depending on the alleged facts in each case, many combinations available which result in an accused being charged with multiple felonies and lesser misdemeanors growing out of the same event. Using the Robbery 1st degree indictment as an example, if an accused were to "gamble" and proceed to a jury trial, it is quite possible (indeed, probable) that he could be convicted on each and every count of the indictment and face many years in prison if the sentences were fixed to run consecutively instead of concurrently on each count. In some states the Robbery 1st degree count *alone* would warrant a sentence of up to thirty years. But typically in Metropolitan Court, if an accused has had no prior record and if he has capably performed the defendant role, he probably will receive a lesser plea of, let us say, a misdemeanor such as simple assault or petit larceny.

The impulse to seek a negotiated plea at this point, in view of the dire possibilities of going to trial and losing, is almost impossible for an accused to overcome. The "benefits" and advantages of a lighter sentence for a lesser plea, or even the possibility of a suspended sentence, become overwhelmingly attractive. For example, the possibilities of a defendant being placed on probation are far greater if he has pleaded to a lesser offense, rather than having been convicted after a trial. An accused's fears of harsh treatment if he does not plead are hardly groundless, considering what courts and judges do to defendants who remain recalcitrant and go to trial.

The jury system and the multiple indictment, then, are used as the initial blows to further collapse an accused's will to resist at this phase of his processing. The district attorney is the moving force, the upper of the millstones, as we have indicated, between which the defendant is ground. The prosecutor calls all the strategic plays:

(1) He decides when the case will appear on the calendar for any particular stage of the proceeding.

(2) He recommends the amount of bail, if any is to be granted (although final discretion is up to the judge).

(3) He selects the particular term or part—that is, which judge will hear or try the case.

(4) He has virtually complete discretion as to whether to prosecute and on what legal grounds (of course, subject to restriction of law).

(5) He often determines what lesser plea, if any, will be accepted in lieu of the case going to trial.

This last prerogative is the most important weapon in the prosecutor's arsenal, for it furnishes his basis for power in negotiations with the significant "others" in the court.

Of intimate concern to the prosecutor are pressures from those with whom he lives in a virtually symbiotic professional relationship in order to maintain his own organizational equilibrium. Thus, although the prosecutor has many powers and prerogatives, and possesses the initiative at virtually all times, he nevertheless depends upon the close, continuing help of the police, judges, lawyers, and other lesser functionaries to attain his ends. And they in turn depend upon him for the identical objectives they desire, namely, as few trials as possible.

Besides the time, energy, and resources that the court organization is reluctant to expend on trials, as a bureaucracy it is loath to engage in activity whose predictability it is unable to control. The rational component of formal organization avoids the fortuitous, the random, and the contingent, such as a jury trial. Greater faith is placed upon symbiotic relationships and structured expectancies to meet the individual and group needs of the court participants, rather than a working through of legal abstractions such as due process. The deviant or even maverick individual who predicates his official conduct solely on accepted notions of due process, or chooses possibilities of action which run counter to normatively established routines, is quickly isolated, neutralized, or re-socialized.

Professionals of the older variety (for example, lawyers) or of the "new" professions (for example, social workers, probation officers, psychologists), have increasingly become part of an occupational mass known as a "salariat," employed and seeking employment in large-scale organizations. This development has created conflict between the professionally oriented individual who seeks satisfaction and recognition outside the immediate, narrow confines of his organization, and the specific task requirements of his organization. Two types of professionals emerge: the "cosmopolitan" seeks satisfaction and recognition outside the organization; the "local" perfects his relationships and rituals within the organization. The "local" develops a method of organizational maneuver, promoting at all times his idiosyncratic career interests but at the same time showing a seemingly passionate, loyal concern for the organization. His "career" rises or falls with the organization, in contrast to the "cosmopolitan," whose interests range beyond the organization— even though he may be just as zealously concerned with career escalation.

Those professionals in the court, such as probation officers, psychologists, and psychiatrists, who believe they will manipulate the legal structures in line with their orientations, discover too late that they are mere instruments to be utilized for larger organizational ends. They find that their body of professional skills cannot be autonomously employed but must be exercised within the framework of precise organizational limits and objectives.

THE "MORAL CAREER"
OF AN ACCUSED PERSON

The vested interest of the district attorney and the police, and their role as agents, is readily perceived and understood by an accused person. He will have sensed certain negative attitudes toward police and will have internalized them long before he has ever been arrested. The agent-mediator roles of judges, lawyers, probation officers, psychiatrists, and members of his own family are not so easily understood. The accused could reasonably define them as allies.

But some of the same reasons which serve as the basis for the district attorney's actions apply also to the judge. According to the ideology of the law, the judge is required to be not only impartial but active in seeking out and preserving the rights of all offenders. Nevertheless, he also has a vested interest in a high rate of negotiated pleas. He shares the prosecutor's earnest desire to avoid the time-consuming, expensive, unpredictable snares and pitfalls of an adversary trial. He sees an impossible backlog of cases, with their mounting delays, as possible public evidence of his "inefficiency" and failure. The defendant's plea of guilty enables the judge to engage in a social-psychological fantasy—the accused becomes an already repentant individual who has "learned his lesson" and deserves lenient treatment. Indeed many judges give a less severe sentence to a defendant who has negotiated a plea than to one who has been convicted of the same offense after a trial.

The lawyer, whether a public defender or a privately retained defense counsel, is subject to pressures peculiar to his role and organizational obligations. But ultimately he is also concerned with strategies leading to a plea. Again, impersonal elements prevail—the economics of time, labor, expense, and the commitment of the defense counsel to the rationalistic values of the court organization; the accused who expects a personal, affective relationship with his lawyer is likely to be disappointed. The lawyer "regulars" of Metropolitan Court are frequently former staff members of the prosecutor's office. They utilize the charisma, "know-how," and contacts of their former affiliation as part of their stock in trade. An accused and his kin, as well as others outside the court community, are unable to comprehend the nature and dimensions of the close relations between the lawyer "regular" and his former colleagues in the prosecutor's office. Their continuing colleagueship is based on real professional and organizational needs of a quid pro quo, which goes beyond the limits of an accommodation one might ordinarily expect in a seemingly adversary relationship. Indeed, adversary features are for the most part muted and exist in their attenuated form largely for external consumption. The principals—lawyer and assistant district attorney—rely upon each other's cooperation for their continued professional existence, and so the bargaining between them usually is "reasonable" rather than fierce.

In his relations with his counsel, the accused begins to experience his first sense of "betrayal." He had already sensed or known that police and district attorneys were adversaries, and perhaps even a judge might be cast in such a role, but he is wholly unprepared for his counsel's performance as an agent or mediator.

It is even less likely to occur to an accused that members of his own family may become agents of the court system. Upon the urging of other agents or mediators, relatives may believe they are really helping an accused negotiate the best possible arrangement under the circumstances. Usually the lawyer will activate next of kin in this role, his ostensible motive being to arrange for his fee. But soon counsel will suggest that they appeal to the accused to "help himself" by pleading.

Sooner or later the probation officer becomes an agent in an accused's processing, depending upon when his services are invoked by judicial requisition.

The accused is usually unable to understand that he does not enjoy the worker-client or doctor-patient relationship with these functionaries. On the contrary, their professional services are preempted by the court organization, and they tend to impute primacy to the organization for the content and meaning of their roles. Usually, a defendant speaks much more freely and reveals a good deal more about himself to psychiatrists and probation officers than he would to other agent-mediators. But he can also reveal too much; he overlooks the lack of real confidentiality present in his relationship with them, and this too has consequences in terms of his ultimate disposition. The court organization may rely heavily on probation and psychiatric reports, especially in those cases where there are no other firm or compelling legal, political, personal, or other criteria to use as a basis for disposing of a case. Bear in mind that the justifications and rationales employed by these agents are grounded in a stock of knowledge about the accused that is pre-cast by police and prosecutor, whose objectivity may be problematic. So, to a large extent, probation and psychiatric reports reaffirm and recirculate the same knowledge about the accused originally furnished by police and prosecutor—refurbished in the patois and argot of social work and psychiatry.

The probation officer has an important function as an agent-mediator, especially after the accused has pleaded and has begun to have second thoughts about the matter. This function may be best described as "cooling the mark out." The phrase was originally used to describe that part of a confidence game in which the operatives leave one of their number behind to discourage the victim from going to the police and to help him accept his new social situation. The victim of, let us say, a swindle must be furnished with a set of apologia or rationales so that he can redefine himself in suitable and defensible terms, instead of going to the police to complain. His embarrassment and defeat are assuaged by the operative who is "cooling him." In similar fashion, in other social matrices, losers and defeated persons must be somehow "cooled out" in order to avoid some sort of social explosion. The lawyer, probation officer, psychiatrist, and next of kin perform important "cooling out" functions. Even the police, prosecutor, and judge may occasionally find it necessary to perform such a function as an accused is processed toward a reconceptualization of self, in the course of changing his initial plea of "not guilty" to one attesting guilt.

Operating under the guise of pseudo-democracy, the court organization utilizes manipulation to promote the myth of the court as a meeting ground of "free professionals" in the service of accused clients. The reality of the situation is that the moment organizational assumptions, directives, and goals are questioned by the "free professionals" (lawyers, psychiatrists, and probation officers), their usefulness and loyalty are simultaneously brought into question. Nothing can be more calculated to intimidate those in the court than the threat of sanctions for non-compliance or resistance. A lawyer will be denied the favors of district attorney, judge, probation officer, and others, and the collapse of his practice will be the ultimate result. Probation officers and psychiatrists will find that they too can be subjected to sanctions.

The judge and district attorney in the criminal court resist through legal and informal means any encroachments on their prerogatives, power, and authority by other professionals in the court setting. These wielders of power and authority in the court use manipulation as one of the forms of discipline and control, especially toward those persons who are wont to consider themselves members of an autonomous profession.

The second variation of the rational-legal authority in the court organization is the apparent existence of a built-in obedience factor in men which makes them more tractable and submissive to organizational demands.

Blind obedience, apart from and independent of the usual deference for "rules" and "office," appears to be an important dimension in any system of authority, including rational-legal authority. It is probably very relevant to a punitively oriented organizational setting such as the criminal court.

A third variation of rational-legal authority as it appears in the criminal court is authority by complicity. Its basis is the datum that evasion and outright breach of rules is a universal pattern for the attainment of organizational goals, which could not otherwise be achieved. Heavy work volume, impossible case loads, and unrealistic work schedules exert inordinate pressures for innovation—the search for shortcuts, the use of forbidden procedures and devices, and the like—in order that production norms may be met.

The character and nature of authority by complicity is best revealed by the experience of the "new worker" who appears in the criminal court. All organizations loathe the recruitment of new persons, because of the adjustments, difficulties, and risks involved. The new worker in the court is a threatening person, for he is unsocialized and ignorant of group norms. The probation period which many civil service organizations establish is in reality a period during which they test the mettle of the individual for conformance with official norms. Thus the new worker is always made to adhere rigidly to an onerous, exacting routine and a high standard of work performance no longer expected of other workers. It is not so much a hazing process as a sizing-up, an evaluation period during which supervisors and fellow workers decide whether the new worker can one day be admitted to the complicity of short cuts, illegal methods, and other work "secrets."

THE PRACTICE OF LAW
AS A CONFIDENCE GAME

The real key to understanding the role of defense counsel in a criminal case is the fixing and collection of his fee. It is a problem which influences to a significant degree the criminal court process itself, not just the relationship of the lawyer and his client. In essence, a lawyer-client "confidence game" is played.

In many "server-served" relationships for a fee—which include not only the practice of law, medicine, or dentistry but also plumbing—there is not always a visible end-product or tangible service involved. A plumber, for example, will usually be able to show that he has performed a service by unstopping a drain, repairing a leaky faucet or pipe—and therefore merits his fee. He has rendered a tangible benefit for his client in return for the requested fee. On the other hand, a physician who has not performed some visible surgery or otherwise discernible procedure may be accused by the patient of having "done nothing" for him. Doctors may even prescribe or administer by injection a placebo to overcome a patient's potential dissatisfaction in paying a fee "for nothing."

The lawyer has a special problem in this regard, no matter what his status or prestige. Much legal work is intangible, because it is simply a few words of advice, some preventive action, a telephone call, negotiation of some kind, a form filled out and filed, a hurried conference with another attorney or an official of a government agency, a letter or opinion written, or a countless variety of seemingly innocuous and even prosaic procedures and actions. These are the basic activities of almost all lawyers at all levels of practice. They represent not precise professional skills but rather the acts of a broker, agent, sales representative, or lobbyist. The lawyer pursues someone else's interests and designs.

In a criminal case, the defendant is soon parted from the spoils he may have acquired from his illicit activities. Not infrequently, the returns from his larceny are sequestered by a defense lawyer in payment of fee. Inevitably, the amount of the fee is close to the dollar value of the crime committed. On occasion, defendants have been known to commit additional offenses while at liberty on bail, in order to get money for payment of legal fees. Defense lawyers make sure that even the most obtuse clients know there is a firm connection between fee payment and the zealous exercise of professional expertise, secret knowledge, and organizational "connections" in their behalf. They try to keep their clients at the precise edge of anxiety calculated to encourage prompt payment of fee. The client's attitude in this relationship is often a precarious admixture of hostility, mistrust, dependence, and sycophancy. By playing upon his client's anxieties and establishing a seemingly causal relationship between the fee and the accused's extrication from his difficulties, the lawyer establishes the necessary groundwork to assure a minimum of haggling over the fee and its eventual payment.

The lawyer must then be sure to manipulate the client and stage manage the case so that help and service at least *appear* to be rendered. This is accomplished in several ways. At the outset, the lawyer uses a measure of sales puff which may range from unbounding self-confidence to complete arrogance.

The special complication of the criminal lawyer is that an accused always "loses," even when he has been exonerated by an acquittal, discharge, or dismissal. His hostility is directed, by means of displacement, toward his lawyer, and in this sense a criminal lawyer never really "wins" a case. The really satisfied client is rare, because even an accused's vindication leaves him with some degree of dissatisfaction and hostility. The man who is sentenced to jail may of course be a singularly unappreciative client.

Bearing these attitudes in mind, the criminal lawyer collects his fee *in advance*. Often, because the lawyer and the accused both have questionable designs upon each other, the lawyer plays the confidence game. First, he must arrange for his fee; second, he must prepare his client for defeat (a highly likely contingency) and then, if necessary, "cool him out"; third, he must satisfy the court organization that he has adequately negotiated the plea so as to preclude an embarrassing incident which might invite "outside" scrutiny.

In his role as double agent, the criminal lawyer performs an extremely vital and delicate mission for the court organization and the accused. Both principals are anxious to terminate the litigation with a minimum of expense and damage. No one else in the court structure is more strategically located, more ideally suited to do so than the lawyer. In recognition of this, judges will cooperate with attorneys in many important ways. For example, they will recess the case of an accused who is in jail awaiting plea or sentence if the attorney requests such action. Overtly this may be done for some innocuous and seemingly valid reason, but the real purpose is to permit the attorney to press for the collection of his fee, which he knows he will probably not get if the case is concluded.

Criminal law is a unique form of private law practice. It simply *appears* to be private practice. Actually, it is bureaucratic practice, because of the lawyer's role in the authority, discipline, and perspectives of the court organization. Private practice, in a professional sense, supposedly involves the maintenance of an organized, disciplined body of knowledge and learning; the lawyer is imbued with a spirit of autonomy and service, the earning of a livelihood being incidental. But the lawyer in the criminal court is a double agent, serving higher organizational rather than professional ends. The lawyer-client "confidence game," in addition to its other functions, helps to conceal this fact.

Together, the organizational, occupational, and structural features of the criminal court are formidable. They promote a rational, efficient system of maximum production which will not be easily overcome by additional counsel and similar resources, for they may in turn be absorbed by the organizational structure. The organizational network of the criminal court today stands interposed between the most libertarian rules and the accused person. The rules as enunciated by the Supreme Court are based on the supposed existence of an adversary model of criminal justice, but the adversary ideal is no more. The additional resources and personnel necessary to implement the traditional rules of due process will instead strengthen the *present* system of criminal justice. The bureaucracy will become even more efficient in the production of guilt.

V
The future of
the establishment

It is of course difficult to fully document the growth of a Federal or even combined Federal-State law enforcement establishment. Since ordinary crime has not yet been publicly equated with radicalism or become wholly identified with minority races, such growth may be minimal or even non-existent. Since politics enters at every turn, and politics is at best an unstable enterprise (witness Watergate and a drop in President Nixon's popularity soon after his smashing electoral victory), perhaps there is not much to fear.

Yet, there are trends, both long and short run, which must be examined to determine *which* critical factors—often hidden from public view—may *become* significant. For instance, the March 17, 1973 *New Republic* reported of President Nixon's budget:

> Additional money for the war against drugs abounds in the budget. Within the Office of the President, a special fund for drug abuse prevention which totaled $25 million last year is being increased to $40 million this year. At the Justice Department, an additional $4 million is being pumped into the attorney-general's office to finance two new 'special action offices'—the Office for Drug Abuse Law Enforcement and the Office of National Narcotics Intelligence. The Bureau of Narcotics and Dangerous Drugs within Justice gets a $4 million boost and the Bureau of Customs within the Treasury Department goes up $25 million, much of it earmarked for drug-related inspection and investigation work.

We also learn that F.B.I. expenditures are scheduled to be increased by $16 million (to a total of $366 million), a large part to be devoted to "administering the famous files." United States attorneys are scheduled for another $6 million, and, contrary to several Presidential pronouncements about "new directions" in prison reform, most of the $14 million increase scheduled for Federal prisons is to cover salaries and maintenance of prison facilities. The Law Enforcement Assistance Administration is scheduled to receive an increase of $36 million, and its total funding will be $891 million.

The Law Enforcement Assistance Administration has been heavily criticized for its tendency to fund essentially police-oriented projects and to merely pay for what states and cities have traditionally deemed within their fiscal responsibilities. Talk of tanks for small towns, misspending of funds to benefit politicians and policemen personally (which, of course, somewhat lessens the problem of the use of funds to repress unpopular "minorities"—corruption may yet be a blessing in disguise; it often is) has reached congress and continuing investigation has been undertaken. Mr. Goulden's *Nation* article is the most comprehensive popular attack on LEAA (several books on the subject are scheduled for publication), and several of its points should be stressed. For one, the growth of the establishment may well be the result of both institutional features of the LEAA program—for instance, most state advisory boards which determine the projects to be funded are composed of law enforcement officials—and a sense of shared values which may be engendered by participation in the program. If policemen do share inchoate values about the nature of society, the nature of crime, the nature of crime control, and their own expertise in dealing with all of these problems, an agency such as LEAA may well serve to air and make legitimate those views and create a sense of unity and identity. Policemen have used professionalism first as a shield against partisan political control, second as a cloak with which to insulate themselves from public scrutiny, and now perhaps as a sword to influence public acceptance of their perceptions. As we know, the public has been receptive, under various circumstances—in narcotics control for instance—and a massive fear of crime may well increase public embrace of these values. The ambivalence of the American people toward crime may well be resolved by acceptance of repression as the first line of defense with only lip service to fundamental social change as the long run solution. Both the pessimism of Goulden and the optimism of Jerris Leonard, Director of LEAA, constitute significant evidence that the attempt is being made. As Leonard put it in an interview, "I am convinced that in a relatively short period of time there will be an entirely new approach to corrections in this country—*and LEAA is going to see to it that there is.*" Although the program he is discussing may well be laudable (from the point of view of fundamentally redefining punishment and corrections, it clearly is not), the disposition of LEAA to become a leader may have important (and dire) social consequences.

It is even conceivable that the degree of cooperation between local police and federal agencies (hampered in the past somewhat by Hoover's imperious tactics) may well substitute for the dreaded "National Police" we all fear. In short, the net result of the New Federalism—and the ever increasing funding for LEAA, the "political" orientation of LEAA, the increasing participation by policemen in political affairs (combined with their desires for unaccountability in police affairs—a curious mixture)—may well create several dragnet local police forces (not necessarily "local" since police centralization is itself occurring) and the presence of one or more National Police forces, all in substantial agreement on goals and methods. Increasing cooperation must inevitably lead to increasing cohesion and an increasing sense of joint enterprise. The moral entrepreneurship of a Harry Anslinger in 1937 may be deemed by historians to be petty in light of developments of the '70's and '80's.

chapter eight

Feeding at the federal trough

JOSEPH C. GOULDEN

Its original good intentions notwithstanding, the federal government has taken the first dangerous steps toward transforming the United States into a society whose police agencies have a repressive capacity unparalleled in history.

The responsible organization, by default as much as by design, is the Law Enforcement Assistance Administration (LEAA), a little-known but fast-growing division of the Justice Department, created by the Omnibus Crime Control and Safe Streets Act of 1968. LEAA's purpose, when conceived by Atty. Gen. Ramsey Clark, was to improve America's chaotic criminal justice system at all levels—arrest, trial, incarceration and release. The Safe Streets Act, Clark told a Senate committee, "is the one appropriate way the federal government can make a major difference. It is based on the demonstrated need for more resources, better applied, to improve the estate of criminal justice in America."

In fact, however, the LEAA has become a pork barrel whose chief beneficiaries are the uniformed police. A vast amount of money is involved. Judging by procedures thus far, the bulk of it will flow directly to the police. In 1969, 59.3 cents of every LEAA action-grant dollar went for police functions; in 1970, 51 cents. Courts, corrections, juvenile delinquency, received minute dabs of cash.

LEAA disburses most of its funds in the form of block grants to the states, which spend the money as they wish, within wondrously broad guidelines. And the ways they are spending federal dollars—

Editor's title. This essay was originally titled "The Cops Hit the Jackpot." From *The Nation,* November 23, 1970. © 1970 by *The Nation.* Reprinted by permission of the publisher.

with federal blessing—raise serious questions about the future of criminal justice in the United States.

In the name of "law and order," LEAA is providing local police with sophisticated "crime prevention" hardware and with techniques developed by many of the same specialists who put men on the moon. The purpose is to curb robberies, burglaries and violent street crimes. The result, however, enables police to keep citizens— the innocent and the guilty alike—under electronic and photographic surveillance while they are shopping, walking public streets, driving automobiles, and visiting both private and public buildings.

In the name of "civil tranquillity," Washington is banding state and local police into compacts to cope not only with violent disorders but also with peaceful protests against defects in American education, foreign policy and racial equality. With federal dollars, the police are constructing massive computerized "intelligence systems" intended to predict unrest—through inputs of information on where citizens travel, what they say, with whom they meet.

The police are being armed to the teeth. For $16,464, LEAA bought the tank that Louisiana police used on September 15 to storm a Black Panther headquarters in New Orleans; the same tank had been used earlier against demonstrating black college students. Pick a state at random. Colorado: 165 riot helmets, 126 gas masks, 118 riot batons, seventy-six cases of Mace, 500 pairs of plastic handcuffs (cheaper than the metal variety, thus useful in mass arrests), thirteen shotguns, three pepper fog machines, with both smoke and gas mixes, four grenade launchers, ninety-four smoke and gas grenades, projectiles, launching cartridges and flares; thirty-three "riot shields," twenty pairs of riot coveralls and gloves. Asking for even more such stuff in 1970, Colorado complained that police lacked equipment in "counties and towns which have college, migrant or minority populations. . . ."

LEAA is strengthening the police politically as well as physically, for "professionalism" gives the cops an aura of infallibility when they deal with lay politicians. Traditionally isolationist and elitist, the cop is using his new wealth to withdraw even further from the restraints of elective government.

In the name of President Nixon's "new federalism," Washington is yielding control of millions of federal tax dollars to police-dominated "state planning agencies."

"Congress passed a 'Safe Streets' program. The states turned it into a 'Safe Pastures' program." This bitter comment comes from a middle-level LEAA official, a holdover from the Ramsey Clark days, who is now seeking work elsewhere. A blatant example of the LEAA pork barrel in action is to be found in Michigan. Grand Rapids, with a population of 200,000 and a police budget of $2.9 million, had through mid-1970 received one LEAA grant: $188 for a 75 per cent share of two Polaroid cameras and a fingerprint kit. Another Michigan town, of 7,500 population, got during the same period $1,650 for an infrared scanning device, $1,275 for a surveillance camera, and $2,400 for basic radio equipment. A National League of Cities survey of mayors found similar discrepancies in a number of other states.

FEDERAL FUNDS AND LOCAL JUSTICE

The LEAA experiment is vital for yet another reason: it could be the last chance for local law enforcement in the United States. Former LEAA administrator Rogovin in 1969 told a convention of the International Association of Chiefs of Police, the leading police professional group: "The American people are concerned—aroused—about crime. They are afraid. If you do not mobilize yourselves to earn [their] support, it will fade. What will happen then? The American people will not tolerate failure. *If local law enforcement fails, then something else will replace it.*"

Another conservative fear was that the federal government would use LEAA as a means to get blacks into segregated police agencies. States a person who worked on the legislation: "Law enforcement today is a white man's profession. McClellan, Hruska and Thurmond feared that if the federal government got into this field, it would give Washington a club over employment practices. Direct federal programs would soon result in federal requirements that law-enforcement agencies stop discriminating."

McClellan asked Clark during judiciary committee hearings whether LEAA would require grant recipients "to have a ratio of police personnel according to race corresponding to the racial population of the area covered by the plan. . . . Would you be able to say under this bill, 'You have got to have 50 per cent of your policemen colored, otherwise you get no money . . . ?' " Clark replied: "We would be required by the law to see to it that funds expended under this Act were not used to further discrimination." The final version of the Act prohibits LEAA from conditioning a grant upon adoption of a "percentage ratio, quota system, or other program to achieve racial balance or to eliminate racial imbalance in any law enforcement agency." This language is the price the Johnson administration paid for passage of the Safe Streets Act— and it is why LEAA must deal with such racist bodies as the Mississippi Highway Patrol. (Mississippi's own 1970 grant application, submitted under the signature of Kenneth W. Fairly, executive director of the state's Division of Law Enforcement Assistance, recognizes that the highway patrol "represents in the Negro mind another repressive force of the white community," and that although it is "an all-white institution . . . it is acknowledged by most people concerned that no significant effort has been made to integrate the patrol.")

THE COPS MOVE IN

Daniel Skoler, director of LEAA's Office of Law Enforcement Planning (OLEP), which processes both block and discretionary grants, says that when the state governments got wind of the Safe Streets money they "responded . . . with the zeal of ballplayers just offered cold beer." And, unfortunately, with about as much coordination.

"What Congress envisioned was a process through which local requirements would filter up to the top and be put into one big mosaic by the state planning agency," says a former Congressional aide involved in writing the Safe Streets Act. "Congress had confidence in local government; it also felt the states would be strong enough to bring all these ideas together into a kind of meaningful plan."

In fact, however, most of the State Planning Agencies and the 450-odd regional planning groups created under their auspices are dominated by law-enforcement agencies. The International City Management Association, in a late 1969 survey, found that only 13 per cent of the members of the SPAs were local policy-making officials, and that only 15 per cent were classed as "citizens" representative of the general community. The rest were either state or law-enforcement functionaries.

The result is that reform of the criminal justice system has become the responsibility of persons with institutional loyalties to the existing system. Few outside voices are present to suggest fundamental changes in the way things are done. Cop rule does not contribute to developing a meaningful "comprehensive" plan, but it does insure that rural counties and hamlets enjoy disproportionate access to the police pork barrel.

At the regional level, the law-enforcement weight is often even heavier. In Florida, each of the seven regional boards is composed of four police chiefs, four sheriffs, a fiscal officer and a hired planner. A Georgia official, responding to a National League of Cities/U.S. Conference of Mayors survey, said regional boards there are picked by "political philosophy rather than competence."

Cities receive short shrift in many states. New York State's SPA has twenty-seven members, only nine of them from New York City (the police commissioner and Dist. Atty. Frank Hogan). Gary, largest city in Indiana, is not represented on the Indiana State Criminal Justice Planning Agency.

FEEDING THE COMPUTERS

"The year past was an excellent one for the vendors of electronic equipment," stated an LEAA internal document circulated in July. "Communications and information systems alone accounted for more than $20 million within the police programs area," one of the OLEP divisions.

As an LEAA official somewhat testily replies, $20 million is a mere tinkle of coins for the mammoth electronics industry. Nonetheless, it is $1 of every $9 of LEAA's total action-grant budget of $182.75 million for 1970. Further, according to one authoritative estimate, spending for electronic gear in other areas—computerized "intelligence systems" for civil disorders and organized crime, and command and control gear—push the overall electronic budget to nearly $50 million. Garlan Morse, president of the Sylvania Electric Products division of General Telephone and Electronics Corporation, predicted to *The New York Times* in April that law-enforcement agencies will be spending $500 million a year on electronic gear by 1975. Morse credits LEAA pilot projects with starting the boom.

That LEAA has no precise figures on how much of its money

on p. 138

goes for electronics is a comment on how little LEAA actually knows of what the states are doing in the field.

A recent LEAA document said the "explosive growth of computerized information systems" was one of the "most dynamic areas in law-enforcement and criminal justice" at all levels—police, corrections, courts, parole, probation and prosecution. More than thirty states, plus the District of Columbia, are developing state-wide systems, a threefold increase since LEAA began funding such projects. Further, LEAA reports:

Many small police departments and sheriffs' offices now have or will have immediate access to vital information through terminals on state networks. A rapidly growing number of cities and urban counties are developing computer systems for law enforcement. Regional systems comprising several units and levels of local government are emerging.

All of the state systems, LEAA says, "are designed to interface with the FBI's National Crime Information Center (NCIC) and several systems will be linked to those in adjoining states. . . . Almost all city and regional systems are interfaced with their respective state system where they exist. . . . In all states, the initial emphasis has been on police applications. . . ." The computers are linked physically by Bell System long-distance wires and microwave transmitters. TV-type display screens are replacing manual terminals for print-outs of transmitted data.

Police are finding a variety of information to put into these computers. One "organized crime" set up in New England is loaded with material on Mafia figures. Juveniles who get into trouble in the San Francisco Bay Area land in the computers (officials say they can "clear the innocent" more quickly when a youngster has a scrape away from his home community). A system based in Florida is intended to log suspected mob figures in and out of Caribbean islands known to be targets of organized crime. Bankruptcy data, business foreclosures, commercial frauds—these and more are going into the computer tapes.

In addition to financing local and state systems, LEAA is directing a project aimed at tying many—and potentially all—of the individual components into a national network. The project is known as SEARCH, an acronym for System for Electronic Analysis and Retrieval of Criminal Histories. The California Council on Criminal Justice (CCCJ) is coordinating SEARCH for LEAA.

Fifteen states are now involved as participants or observers, working with $1,429,460 provided by LEAA and $1,087,368 from state matching funds. Each state is converting 10,000 "criminal histories" into electronically accessible form. The subjects are felons with at least two arrests and one court disposition. Persons involved in SEARCH argue that it is not a national data bank. Nevertheless, a central index, now being developed by the Michigan state police, will be directly available to each state and will contain summary data on each state-held file.

"Anyone who says there aren't privacy issues [in SEARCH] is a goddamned liar," says Charles Rogovin, who was still LEAA administrator when SEARCH began. According to Rogovin, the issue was raised at one of the first SEARCH meetings, at Notre Dame University in early 1969. The decision then was to make data accumulation a state activity, so as to avoid putting too much sensitive information into a central location. Rogovin has mixed feelings on SEARCH: as a professional law-enforcement man, he sees the need for fast, accurate information in an era when criminals can jet across the nation in four hours. He also sees SEARCH as something that could "shape American criminal justice for the next half century"—for good or for evil.

Senator Ervin, although he was not referring directly to SEARCH, expressed his contempt of national data banks in a September 8 speech to the Senate:

The new technology has made it literally impossible for a man to start again in our society. It has removed the quality of mercy from our institutions by making it impossible to forget, to forgive, to understand, to tolerate. . . . The undisputed and unlimited possession of the resources to build and operate data banks on individuals, and to make decisions about people with the aid of computers and electronic data systems, is fast securing to executive branch officials a political power which the authors of the Constitution never meant any one group of men to have over all others.

SEARCH, when operative, will make police files instantaneously interchangeable. And many of the states involved in SEARCH are coincidentally developing computerized intelligence systems for material far removed from violent crime: "to analyze the potential for disorders," as stated in an LEAA internal document. The California Council on Criminal Justice, fascinated by the wonders of electronics, describes its desired system as follows:

The state will have an operating intelligence system for the collection, analysis, interpretation, and dissemination of information relative to the prediction, detection, prevention, suppression and control of riots and disorders. This system will provide for necessary exchange of information at state and local levels, thus furnishing urgent and necessary coordination and co-operation.

Similar language is found in other state comprehensive plans. The type of intelligence useful to such systems is "raw" in the purest, or foulest, sense of the word. It deals with the political attitudes and activities of persons motivated by a diversity of reasons. Legitimate dissenter and terrorist will go on the tapes together.

SEARCH's mere existence, in an era of intensifying national paranoia, is an invitation to abuse. An action brought by the Oklahoma Civil Liberties Union contends that the state's Office of Interagency Coordination has prepared a blacklist of 6,000 Oklahomans who are regarded as "actual or potential troublemakers." The compilation of the list was made possible in large part by a grant of the LEAA in the amount of $29,953.

Still alive is a scheme of the Los Angeles police department (which wants $681,000 in LEAA money) to "develop 'intelligence' indicators of social and community problems that may lead to trouble. . . . This requires a center for receiving, analyzing and interpreting many different and diverse sources of information that might aid materially in the diagnosis of the build-up of social pressures that could possibly lead to a civil disturbance."

AN EYE ON US ALL

Another form of electronic apparatus, equally popular with technology-minded cops, poses a more immediate threat to the privacy of citizens. As is true with much of the new crime-fighting gear being developed in LEAA projects, the stated purpose is laudable; the byproduct is sobering. The equipment in question is cameras—still, movie and television—operated from surreptitious locations as a substitute for or adjunct to police patrols. They are intended to record activities of criminals; unfortunately, they also catch the innocent.

The Wilmington police are also buying an "anti-sniper van" which has photography portholes. In the van are to be four AR-18

.223 caliber rifles, four twelve-gauge shotguns and four .243 caliber carbines, and three tear gas kits, purchased at a cost to LEAA of $2,120. LEAA is also buying the Wilmington cops 1,750 rounds of rifle bullets and 250 rounds of double-ought buckshot, known to law-enforcement specialists as a "killer load."

A surveillance system being developed in Tampa, Fla., uses computers to control a network of video tape recorders and alarms placed in "convenience" grocery stores, overlooking parking lots, and atop warehouses in high-crime areas. STAVS (for Sensitized Transmitted Alarm Video System) is an expanded version of the cameras long used by banks. According to Florida's prospectus, no pictures actually will be made unless a crime is attempted. Activation of the camera then causes broadcast of a prerecorded radio signal to roaming squad cars or helicopters. A high-intensity light comes on atop the target building. The Florida prospectus states:

> The possibility of immediate apprehension of a criminal while in commission of a crime is the ultimate of evidence for prosecution. In the event immediate apprehension is not affected, then the [police] department would have video tape evidence of the crime and positive identification of the culprit while in the act of committing the crime.

Tampa citizens will also be subject to covert surveillance even before they enter a business house. The Florida plan states: "The video-recording camera is installed overlooking a shopping center parking lot. The camera surveillance is watched on monitors. When suspicious activity occurs, the operator can utilize the affected camera's zoom lens for a close-up."

What might the monitors disclose? Teen-agers engaged in innocent afternoon necking; a housewife adjusting her hose; a salesman taking a nap; a businessman using his car for a meeting he wishes to keep secret. All observed on a federally funded candid camera, with close-ups.

Much of LEAA's electronics work is laudable. By cajolery and demonstration, it has convinced police departments that their radios should be compatible with those of neighboring jurisdictions. It is financing research on a compact trans-receiver radio to keep foot patrolmen in contact with precincts. A computerized burglar alarm system in Detroit has cut police reaction time by half.

But what of the other electronic activities—the recordings and photography? What safeguards will protect the American public from police who decide to use this system to transform the United States into a "wired society"? I asked this question of a former LEAA official, a man who supports covert police work. His response wasn't reassuring. "The police," he said, "will be so inundated by information from such systems they won't be able to sort it out. Sure, you'll have thousands of feet of film and tapes, but how are you going to pick out one person and follow him around? What kind of computer could do that?"

ARRESTING THE SYMPTOMS

Judge A. Leon Higginbotham, Jr., vice chairman of the National Commission on the Causes and Prevention of Violence, criticized LEAA's civil disorders work before a House subcommittee last spring. He expressed "great fear . . . that we get more expertise on getting Mace and riot guns than we have on community relations." He noted that the Safe Streets Act "gives a disproportionate advantage if you are chasing riot equipment than if you are working on community relations. I think that somehow or other we have to start turning the corner on that point."

Yet LEAA has been moving in exactly the opposite direction, and at an accelerating pace.

The Justice Department's Community Relations Service, in an unpublished critique circulated last summer, blamed the predominance of police on state and regional planning boards for the slipshod programs drafted by the states. Quotations from two CRS consultants in the Midwest are illustrative:

This program is a one-way street. Demands will be made of citizens. However, there are no admonitions or demands placed upon law-enforcement officials to deal constructively . . . and justly with citizens. . . .

There has been no input from minorities. Crime tremendously affects minorities and jeopardizes the health of these communities.

In 1969 riot-jittery states made heavy allocations of Safe Streets funds for prevention and control of civil disorders—22.5¢ of every dollar. A special section of the Safe Streets Act directed LEAA to make riot grants in advance of approval of state comprehensive plans—a means of getting equipment to cops in a hurry. And much of these funds went for hardware items—tear gas, firearms, protective gear, floodlights, Louisiana's tank (described officially as a command-and-control vehicle). Once the police were armed, however, state interest in civil disorders dropped markedly. In fiscal 1970 the states allocated only 3.9 per cent of their block-grant money for civil disorders. "It's easier to buy a bunch of gas cannisters and masks than to find a sensible way to spend civil disorders money," said an official in LEAA's Western regional office. Yet enough riot money remains to make LEAA a minor bonanza for police hardware manufacturers.

During fiscal 1969, for example, states allocated only 14 per cent of their action grants for corrections. Through vigorous arm-twisting, LEAA managed to get that figure up to 27 per cent in 1970.

A federal role in law enforcement is an irreversible fact. Indeed, a major LEAA worry during the current session of Congress was being appropriated more money than it wanted, a rarity for a federal agency.

But now that the scientists are sniffing around law enforcement, the level of police technology is due for a quantum jump. More and more cops will be attending criminology classes and advanced professional programs under LEAA sponsorship (if only to get away from home for a few weeks), and the universities are recognizing law enforcement as a new area of grantsmanship. (However, Police Chief James Ahern of New Haven, Conn., says this program has "resulted in . . . a crop of new courses designed more to attract federal dollars than to be relevant to the student's needs. The money spent on those efforts has produced a second-rate system that has more training than education. In fact, the police science courses supported have tended to segregate police on campuses and limit severely their educational experience.")

The American people deserve something better for their money. The various Presidential commissions of the mid-1960s—crime, Kerner and violence—said quite specifically that the basic structure of the police agencies is unsound, a condition demonstrated through their failure to perform their basic mission. Nonetheless, LEAA is devoting its energy (and great sums of our money) to buttressing up the existing institution, rather than stepping back for a critical look and asking, "Shouldn't we start from the ground up?"

An example: Asked for a concrete accomplishment of LEAA, Associate Director Coster points to the District of Columbia, whose crime rate has dropped during the past year. LEEA's role was to supply money to increase the police force by 1,000 to 5,100. The conditions that caused the crime remain untouched.

"The LEAA program has no place for anyone with dreams of repression," Richard Velde told an IACP meeting in 1969. "It is designed to make a safer America, a more just America for everybody—black and white, poor and rich." But LEAA has chosen sides; it is a program for cops, not for criminal justice, and the men in charge are insuring that it remains just that.